First Edition 2016

ISBN 978-0-9976105-1-2

Scorpio Press
www.Scorpio.Press

First Edition, [illegible]

ISBN [illegible]

[illegible]

Falling Into Ease
Release Your Struggle
And Create A Life You Love

by
Aliza Bloom Robinson

Index

Forward 11
Introduction 13
Get About the Business of Being You! 17
Innermost Yearnings 20
Suffering Is Not For the Weak of Heart 22
The Triple A's and Triple C's 26
In the Beginning 30
Useless and Unnecessary Suffering. 33
Sub - Layers of the Heart 40
Creating Space 45
Believe it Because We See it?. 51
Or See it Because We Believe it?
A Look at Fear 57
One Key to End All Suffering for All Time 64
A Word About Emotions 69
Finding the Elusive Peace 73
That you Desire and Deserve
Would it be Alright with You if Life Got Easier? 75
The Great Grand Vision. 79
Accessing the Subconscious 85
In the Midst of Life 95
The End 99
If-Only Drain 104
From Separation to Oneness 109
Get Your Gratitude On 115
Why We Are on the Planet 119
Self-Esteem - Coming To Love Yourself 125
Finding Ease in the Better. 132
It's Your Life - When are You Going to Live it?? 138
Closing Thoughts 144
About the Author 149

Forward

This book has come about through my life experiences and my desire to help others. I made a covenant with Spirit back in 1993, to listen and follow. This covenant has led me places I never would have thought or considered. It came out of a very dark place in my life, when everything had fallen apart. I hit my knees and prayed, "I can't do this, I can't manage my own life, help me." The immediate response was something like, "follow me, I will open doorways and pathways, all you have to do is walk through them." My covenant was to do just that; if something appeared for me to do, I would do it. I would take the next step and the next. The way has been a bit windy, (not as in the wind, but as in curvy). I've taken risks and made choices that my friends and family have questioned. I listen deeply to the impulse within me, the guidance being given and to the best of my ability, follow it. The result is that my life is rich beyond measure, deeply meaningful and filled with adventure!

This book is a part of following my covenant. My direct connection with Spirit guides each writing session, each chapter and each book that I write. I have utmost gratitude for the people, circumstances and situations along my path!

It is my hope that the words in this book touch your heart, free your soul and perhaps, even, transform your life.

Introduction

What are you struggling with? Where are you suffering? Would it be alright with you if life got easier? I am Aliza Bloom Robinson, Vibrational Catalyst, and my commitment is to help make your life easier and end your suffering. I've been a minister for over 16 years and walked with people through their journeys from darkest despair and agonizing heartbreak into their highest, joyous celebrations. Life is meant to be good. We are here to make manifest the glory of our Essence, to bring forth the love and light that is inside each one of us. In order to do that we have to surrender, dissolve and otherwise eliminate the dark through this illumination. We can do that and end the struggle and eliminate suffering as we know it, opening the way to a life of greater ease.

I'm so glad you are here. Since you are, I am going to make an assumption about you. Now, I know assumptions are often incorrect, but here it goes anyway. I'm guessing that life is going pretty well and that you would tell anyone you meet that your life is good. Things are not bad, nothing is terribly wrong, but you are carrying a deep dark secret – one perhaps that you haven't even told yourself. That is: You want more. You want more something, maybe you can't even quite name it, but it is there, this little nudge, an impulse, a nagging discontent with how things are. Then you beat yourself up, because, really, your life is not that bad.

I know because I was that person. I had a good life, I had reached most of my dreams and career goals. I lived in a fun city, had a wonderful relationship, made decent money and had great friends. Everything was going along just fine. Then one day, I woke up with something, like a dust cloud over my vision. Like a blah had settled over me. At first it was nothing much, then it began to build.

What is this, I thought? Where did this come from? Over the course of a couple of months I went from being on top of the world to hanging out in the ditches. It was crazy making! Maybe you have experienced something similar.

Because I've spent my entire adult years on a spiritual path, a continual journey of awakening, I became curious. But not before everything fell apart. My work shifted subtly, my relationship became a bit more distant, I was feeling discontent. So I hired a coach to help me see what was happening inside of me.

I discovered that even though my life was fine, it was not deeply fulfilling and I wanted MORE. There was more for me to do and be. The yearning was for a deeper contribution, more purpose, more passion, more connection. The quiet, yet dark cloud of discontent was calling me to not settle for what was, but instead to go for what was possible.

What is the reason you picked up this book? What is calling you? What in your life is ready for an upgrade? What area in your life has worked beautifully in the past but is not its most effective now? Just like when our computers need upgraded. When you bought that brand new computer a few years ago it was the top of the line, but now, it's old, slow and limited compared to what's available today.

Uplevel your life! Read along to make the upgrades in your experience to release suffering and struggle and create the life you love.

We all know there is immense suffering on the planet - it comes in many forms from the poorest, hungry, diseased orphan children in third world countries, to the hungry and homeless in our back yards. It shows up in violence and hatred. It shows up in lack and limitation. It shows up in politics and government. It shows up with disease and tragedy, when we or a loved one gets a medical diagnosis or someone dies.

Given that suffering happens, how can I propose to end struggle and eliminate suffering? The end of struggle and suffering happens first in your own mind, heart and experience. When we end individual struggle, we can help eradicate global suffering. This is what this book is about. The end of suffering, release of struggle and the clarity and pathway to live the life you'd love. It is in a sense, a guide to enlightenment. The first step towards healing or shifting of anything is the acknowledgement and acceptance of it. The world suffers. There is suffering in the world. Let us acknowledge it. Let us accept it, then let us move on to a new experience of ease.

A word about acceptance.
Acceptance is not the same as condoning or supporting. It is a simple, yet powerful principle that eliminates the resistance to a thing that is. Accepting is the first step in spiritual growth.

What is the truth about you? We will deal with the world later, but for now, what's going on with you? What would you love to see change? What is your story about why you don't have what you want and why you can't have what you want? Let's take a look. What is the place in your life that has a little blah hanging over it? Especially that place you think you can't change?

Perhaps it is a job situation that you think you can't leave for x amount of years. Perhaps it is a child or parent challenge that seems to be hovering over you. Perhaps it's money or lack of. Perhaps you know you are called to something different, but have a zillion reasons why you can't answer that calling. Or maybe you've gotten a diagnosis that has tripped you up. What is it that you are struggling with or suffering through? Choose one. You can make a list, but let's focus on only one thing at a time. Look for the deepest one, the core underlying belief that is keeping you stuck where you are.

Are you willing to dive in? Are you willing to look, see, tell the truth and take authentic action? Are you? If so - read on! If not, that's ok, no judgment. Read on anyway and maybe something will jump into your awareness that will end your suffering.

1

Get About the Business of Being You!

Know Thyself. The Ancient Greek aphorism holds as true today as it did in the days of Socrates. Know thyself. You are here to make manifest the glory of God, in you, through you and as you. As you come to know yourself, all aspects of you, you are freed. The way to finding ease and peace comes in discovering that which you love and that which threatens you; that which is your greatest fear and that which is your greatest dream. As you discover and free the deeper places of anger, shame and guilt within you, also find and free your brilliance, genius and passion.

In getting to know thyself, we get to answer the question "Who am I?" My answer to that is: I am funny, sexy, strong and flexible. I am a brilliant light who has tried to dim herself to make others feel better. I can shine it, but I can also hide it. I'm a chameleon, I can fit in, but never really free myself. I like people and I love transformation. I love to be acknowledged and recognized, even as I push it away sometimes. I feel and know Awakening and yet I don't always live from that place. Sometimes, I let life get to me, I complain, I whine and I wallow. Then I stand up and go again.

I've been so emptied out that there was nothing left. I had no feelings, no desires, no worries and certainly no drive. I've been so full, I'm empty. I've touched the heights of bliss and been on my knees in despair. I tell you this because now you know I can relate.

I will show you how to be you, in a very real, expansive way that doesn't make sense to our rational minds.

Who are You?

You are a spiritual being on a journey to remember Wholeness. You are here with an amazingly full tool box of opportunities, gifts, challenges and potential. You are here to find joy and love and peace. Who doesn't want more peace in their lives? Who doesn't want more light and love and ease in their lives? Who doesn't want more play and fun and delight?

The thing is that sometimes we think these things are too far away, unreachable or some other really false idea that keeps us stressed and in struggle and suffering. Who are you, as you read this book? What are your hopes and dreams? Where and how do you stay mired in suffering or stuck in the ruts of your life? There is no judgment here, only query.

As you begin to see the patterns, to discover the places that bind you tight, you can begin to unravel them.

What would you love instead of struggle? Can you put a name to it? Can you allow a picture to emerge, one that has you living life fully? Begin that now. What would you love instead of suffering?

I'm here to guide you to your own experience of Oneness. Once you touch it, you'll want it. Once you want it, you will be guided to surrender into it.

Surrender into Oneness, surrender into Love, surrender into Wholeness, surrender into You! You can do this by letting go and releasing all that no longer serves you, all that is unlike love, all that keeps you bound in your humanity.

But isn't our humanity what we are here to embrace? Yes, of course. And in the embrace of it, we accept it, allow it and integrate it. It's quite beautiful, actually. When we embrace our humanity fully, we realize our divinity. For we discover our divinity in the midst of humanity. They are not separate. They are not mutually exclusive. They are the paradox resolved, the entire spectrum of polarities as one.

2

Innermost Yearnings

What does your inner heart long for? What is the yearning in the depths of you? Is it so faint that you don't even know? Or is it screaming so loudly you can hear nothing else? Take a moment to quietly listen. Take the time to pay attention. Quit trying to make it go away with your excuses and reasons, and jabbering about why it isn't important or even valid to listen to your heart.

The deepest longing that we have as humans is connection. It might be your deepest longing or it might not, but as a culture, connection is what we are missing and yearning for. We want to get married then divorced, we want to live with others, then alone, we want friends then we want them to go away. What is this push pull that so many people experience?

It is, in its deepest core the desire for soul connection. We are spiritual beings here on planet earth having a human experience.

Over the millennia, humanity has mastered the illusion of separation. At some level our egoic collective made up a story that we are separate and that we have to go it alone in order to prove ourselves. This illusion was created with the desire to be independent. Over time, we forgot that separation was an illusion, was an act;

we believed so much in our belief that we became blind to the Truth, that we could never be separate from that which sourced us.

Think about our teenagers who so desperately want to prove themselves on their own terms. It was sort of like that.

That which sourced us is God, Spirit, Creation, the Universe itself; use whatever term works for you. We are Creation creating itself. We are the individualized expression of Creation, and we are Creation.

I used to say to my clients and congregations, "In God we live and move and have our being. Equally important, through us, God lives and moves and has expression." I believe this to be true, however, I currently substitute the word Creation for God. For me, the words Creation, Spirit, Source or the Universe are better representations of that which we call God than the word God. They have more expansion and are more open to interpretation.

3

Suffering is Not for the Weak of Heart

My friend, Irene has just had her knee replaced. There is no doubt that she is in physical pain right now. She says, surgery was fine, but recovery is not for sissies. Within the physical pain, there is the relative torture of physical therapy, there is recovery from the procedure she went through to remove the damaged portion of her leg and to replace the bones with something else. There is the adjustment time, when the body goes through "what is this foreign thing in my leg and what happened to my parts?"

There is the emotional process of being in recovery, of working through the time that it takes to heal and in the process of moving forward. There is the spiritual process of allowing, accepting that there is a new knee in place and that there is nothing wrong. She didn't fail, she isn't broken, even as her body is undergoing medical treatment to fix a problem. That doesn't mean she is broken or there is anything wrong with her.

I was working with a woman recently who was struggling and suffering with a physical issue. She was unraveling the belief that since there was something wrong with her physically, that must mean there was something wrong with her spiritually. Guess what I said? "NO! One has nothing to do with another."

Yes, there might have been some thoughts that lead to a physical manifestation, but there also might not have been. Metaphysics in the recent decades has been useful for many people and many ailments in changing a thought to change a manifestation. But it has also been used against us in what I call metaphysical malpractice.

I have seen many people use tools like Louise Hay introduced in the 70s in her book *You Can Heal Your Life*. These are wonderful tools to use on yourself. Ask yourself the question, "Is there something that I'm thinking or doing that may be contributing to the cause of this current situation?" Often there is.

However, these tools are never, ever to be used against yourself or another person. If Louise says that negative thinking causes cancer and you get a diagnosis of cancer then someone comes to you and says something like, "I knew you would get cancer, you are always so negative," it's not helpful. Do you see how that is malpractice? It is wrong. Use it for yourself, ask yourself the questions, "Is there a place I can do something differently? Is there something I need to see here, to heal here?" Use it if it is expansive and helpful. If it's not, don't worry about it.

We do not have 100% control over the things that happen in our lives. We do have 100% control over how we respond to it.

When my friend's knee was going out, she was worried that she did something wrong. Do you do that when your favorite shirt gets a tear in it? Or a favorite necklace breaks? Do you take that personally? No, of course not. Do we worry about what we did that was wrong when a tire goes flat on our car? Or the battery goes dead or a belt breaks? No!

Life happens. The question is how are you going to stand in it? What are you going to do now, given that this is happening? Is the thing that is happening calling you to a new awareness? Is it pushing up against a belief or pattern that is ready to be changed?

I twisted my ankle when I was in Bali. I went down off a curb and knew that I had injured myself. My response was, "Oh that hurt and it's going to hurt for a while." What I did was go about and enjoy my trip to the best of my ability while at the same time adding an ice and bandage routine to the mix. What I didn't do was beat myself up about it or worry or fret or spin my wheels in why did this happen to me? I don't know why it happened. It sucked at one level and on another it just was what it was.

Today, almost 10 weeks later, my ankle is still fussing with me and it turns out I tore a ligament, so now I get to do something different in my treatment of it, because it is not healing the way I want it to. Does that make me wrong? Or broken? Or spiritually deficient somehow? No, it does not. Does it make me frustrated? Yes, and perhaps that frustration will lead me to the next steps that will promote healing.

There is nothing wrong with you. You might have a bodily ill or issue. But that is your body - ***you are not your body.***

You have a body. That is all. Take care of it to the best of your ability and when something goes amiss, fix it.

You are perfect, whole and complete, no matter what your current life situations are. Do your best to lay down suffering and go about your business.

I have friends who have died of cancer, who have had accidents or situations that have left them crippled in body. Does that affect their wholeness? Not in spirit. When you begin to shift your identity from the outer expression to that which is deep within, nothing else matters.

Yes, you get to deal with life. Yes, you get to manage what life gives you. Back in 2000, when I was ordained, I thought that I wouldn't have life challenges any more, (a bit facetiously, I will admit). Now that I'd arrived and been anointed, life would get simpler and easier. Instead, I have found that hasn't been the case at all. I thought I would be able to walk on water, that life would work itself around me, that I could stay in the peaceful eye of the storm at all times. Not so much. I can't walk on water now, even when it's frozen. I slip and slide as much or more than the next person.

4

The Triple A's and Triple C's

In the financial world of stocks and bonds, there are ratings. The AAA rating is excellence, the highest quality you can buy. And the CCC bonds are junk bonds. Almost not worth wasting your time and money.

In life we can find the same ratings. When we live a AAA life, things are good, the best they can be. The energy flows, happiness happens, abundance and health show up in greater ways. Life flows better. Here's why. When the Triple A's are activated, physically in our bodies all the valves are open and we are operating with all cylinders firing.

Our bodies are channels for our experiences--not the woo-woo channeling, as in something outside of us coming through us, but physical channels for our life experience. When we are able to clear the channel by removing blocks and obstacles and closing leaks and gaps, the energy flows better. Picture a huge garden hose with a 6-inch diameter. Sometimes the hose gets kinked to where there is a trickle of water flowing through or sometimes the flow stops completely. Sometimes, the hose gets something in it, like a pebble, a small animal, a bunch of leaves stopping the flow, or anything that works like a dam within it. Sometimes the hose gets a hole in it, perhaps a pinhole or a long knife type cut. Either way, the flow is hampered.

It is the same with our physical bodies. We are energy bodies; life is energy itself flowing in and through our physical body. When we are clear and clean, whole and centered life flows fully and freely. When we get stuck, shut down, or off center, we shut down the flow. Like the hose, we can have obstacles show up that work like a dam, or we get a leak or kink in our flow. Anytime this happens and the energy doesn't flow freely, symptoms show up.

The Triples A's are Appreciation, Allowing and Accepting. When we live in appreciation, allowing and accepting what is, life flows. When the A's are not active, the C's show up.

The Triple C's are Complaining, Criticizing and Condemning. Remember the C's are the junk bonds. When we live in the C's, we get junk life. The C's themselves are obstacles, blocks and leaks in our energy field and body temple. The C's keep us stuck in the lower half of our body, with only a trickle of life force able to reach the upper body. Feel the C's right now. Feel what happens when you activate the C's. Notice that you feel heavy, uninspired and weary. The challenge with the C's, is that once they are activated they take over. When you begin to complain, what do you get more of? Things to complain about.

Triple A's and Triple C's
Appreciation, Allowing, Accepting
Complaining, Criticizing, Condemning

Did you ever have a bad day, where you woke up on the wrong side of the bed, and things went from bad to worse all day long? Of course, we all have had those days. What do most of us do then? We complain, or we criticize or we condemn. The C's are like a virus. Once brought into the open air, it is catching and very contagious.

You could try it as an experiment, but I'd recommend trying the A's as an experiment instead. Simply put, the C's block the flow of life and the A's bring about the flow of goodness and wellbeing.

The Golden Rule

What you do to others, you do to yourself. It's a basic life principle, what goes around comes around. When you treat others with kindness, you receive kindness. When you are generous, you see and receive generosity. When you are mean and critical, that's what you receive in return. Said another way - what you believe is what you see. If you believe in lack, you see lack. If you believe in fear and corruption, that is what you will see in the world.

What if you could begin to believe in Love? What if you could begin to believe in You? What if you could begin to believe in Good?

When you give the A's, Appreciation, Allowing and Accepting to another, you really are giving them to yourself. When you hand out the C's, (complaining, criticizing and condemning) you also are giving those to yourself.

We are only One, there is only One of Us. We are humanity, each an individualized expression, unique in our personality and traits, but One together. All of life is a mirror. What do you see? What would you like to see?

Where in your life would you like to see a change?

There is brilliance in the universe. There is also pain and suffering. In which would you rather hang out? Could you accept and allow every feeling you had? Could you accept and allow every thought that is flowing through your mind to flow? What if in the accepting of the pain and suffering, there comes a new found freedom, one that is free of suffering and opens the pathways to love?

Drop the resistance. Come into Allowing. Enter into the mystical, magical moment of now. Free from the past and the future. This moment is right here, come on in.

We are here on this planet to live life to its fullest. When we get to the end of our lives, research says, it is loving and experiencing and relationships that matter. Regrets, if there are any, are about not living life fully, not going after dreams, not telling people how much they meant to us.

5

In the Beginning

In the beginning when there was nothing at all, there came an impulse that was so great that something happened. It was the beginning of life as we know it. It was the beginning of our evolving nature. First there was light, then a firmament, the foundation for all that will come. Then the sun and moon, day and night, land and sea. There were the plants and animals and then there was us. It could be said that evolution ended with us, except we continue to evolve as humanity and as souls.

The time has come for another quantum leap. One that will shift us from living in the dream of the illusion of separation into the Truth of Oneness. In this leap, we leave behind separation and all of its corresponding traits and qualities and move into something new.

Let's back up for a moment. With each step of creation there was a critical moment - a moment when the current life could no longer survive as it was, there was an impulse that became so great that a quantum leap happened. Wallace Wattles, in his book, *The Science of Getting Rich*, says, "When an organism has more life than can be expressed in the functions of its own place, it develops the organs of a higher plane, and a new species is originated."

Simply put, when any particular organism gets to the point that their existence is in question something has to happen. They could either adapt and change or die. Life has to change.

Now we are coming to a critical moment; there is a closely approaching critical mass that will cause the leap into our next generation and expression. Think about our world for a moment - it is crazy right now. Global warming, disease, fighting, hunger, gangs, killings, wars and politics. Yikes! Do we have a chance for survival?

Yes, we do! Our chance for survival is in finding ourselves again. It is in listening to the deepest impulses that are wrangling to get our attention. It is in this leap in consciousness that we enter into a new awareness. It is a coming home to the new. It is a returning to the Truth, a letting go of all illusions and false beliefs. In the new, there will be no fear, no fighting, no lack and no suffering. There will be only Love, Acceptance, Compassion and Oneness.

There was a movement a few years back where teachers in two fighting countries introduced their students to each other. They got to know each other through letter writing and Facebook. They walked away from fear and into each other's hearts. The premise is that if we actually knew each other, it would be much harder to kill each other.

Greg Boyle, Founder of Homeboy Industries, found the same thing. When he was first ordained he was sent into a rough area of Los Angeles, CA. It was drug and gang infested with many rival gangs. The crime was horrific, the nerves tense, the fear high. It was in this environment that Greg began to head out into the streets. He became a presence. He would get out on his bicycle and travel around speaking to anyone who came into his path, saying hello and simply being around. Over time, they began to trust him. Over more time, he has virtually eliminated all gang activity and crime in the neighborhood. He set up many programs, each one coming from a direct need that he encountered. He valued each person, he met them where they were and he helped them. He created opportunities for rival gang members to work together side by side. They discovered love. They discovered they were the same. They laid down their weapons and their fear and their rage and began to better themselves. Read his book, *Tattoos on the Heart* which is filled with antidotes and heart wrenching stories of awakening and healing and the transformation of one of the harshest communities in the country.

How did he do this? It came by honoring, valuing and modeling love. It came through his deep commitment that each person matters. That every human life is important and every person has gifts to give. He transformed a neighborhood wrought with rage and fear into a healthy community. It was not without its challenges and you can still find remnants of the way it was, but the transformation is beautiful to behold.

6

Useless and Unnecessary Suffering

Did you know that suffering lives in and through us, but it is not real? I don't mean to say that if you are currently suffering, that your pain is not real. However, suffering lives only in our minds. If we had no judgment or story about that which we are suffering over, it would cease to be.

Suffering is a mental exercise, a mental figment or construct. Some of us learned suffering more than others. Some of us came in with a deep attachment to suffering. Like suffering makes life worthwhile. "If you aren't suffering, you aren't doing life right." What are your unconscious voices around suffering? Where do they show up in your life? Take a moment to list some out.

Drop into a deeper place in your awareness and ask yourself what you are carrying about suffering? What are the stories, the lines, the beliefs you have about suffering? Are they sentences like: "If you aren't suffering, you aren't doing enough" or "life is tough and we have to suffer." If this is pushing your buttons and you are in resistance to the conversation here, take a breath and see if you can open into the possibility that you don't have to suffer quite so much.

Life on planet earth is a fascinating journey and it is filled with adventures and experiences. We don't always get to choose what happens and sometimes, as I like to say, "Life Happens." Life has inherent with it a certain degree of struggle and even suffering. When a loved one dies, we typically suffer. When we are hurt we typically suffer.

Life is filled with suffering and your work is to separate the necessary from the unnecessary suffering.

A teacher of mine in seminary, Rev. Ed Rabel, taught life is filled with suffering and your work is to separate the necessary from the unnecessary suffering. Consider the ways that you suffer in your life either now or in the past. There is a sense of suffering that some of us put on like a mantel, wearing it proudly and almost like a badge of honor.

There are many ways to suffer and I'm here to tell you that you can end all of your useless and unnecessary suffering. I will also present the possibility that you can eliminate what has been called necessary suffering as well.

A short list of the ways people suffer:

- Grief
- Time lack
- Lack of money
- Not living the life of their dreams
- Bosses - other people
- Working for a living - rather than living for life
- Self esteem
- Worthiness
- Guilt

- The if only syndrome
- Feeling separate
- Alone and lonely
- Dried up inside
- Is this all there is???
- What's the point?
- Not believing

What if suffering was simply a vehicle or trigger for evolution? What if your suffering could really be used for your greater good? Some suffering can be used, other suffering can be dropped and transformed.

You are NOT Broken!
There is NOTHING Wrong with You!
You might have some physical or emotional issues, but that doesn't have anything to do with the Truth of who you are. You might even have some spiritual issues, but that also does not mean there is something wrong! It only means you have issues you get to stand in and walk through. That's all.

Life is about coming to Love. Coming to acceptance. Life is life on this planet. We are given a body; we are given life circumstances based on whatever... life lessons, karma, soul agreements... who knows for sure. I think all of those are valid at some level, but the point for today is this: Whatever life gives you, face it, look it in the eye, make a conscious choice about how you are going to walk through it and then let it be.

We fuss and muss and worry so much that we make mountains out of anthills. There is nothing wrong! You can't do it wrong! And you'll never get it "done," so relax. It's all right.

One of my favorite lines of all times comes from the movie "*The Best Exotic Marigold* Hotel". The hotel manager says to a guest,

***"Everything will be alright in the end.
If it's not yet alright, no worries,
it's not yet the end."***

My Heart is Breaking, What Do I Do?

Heart Break comes in many ways: the breakup of a relationship or the loss or death of a loved one or pet or job, even. Heartbreak always revolves around loss of something we are attached to, like a job or something physical, or emotional. When we get attached to something and then lose the attachment, it causes a ripping, like Velcro being ripped apart. My heart has been broken more than once. I've lived in and through heart break, through loss and also through challenge.

Our hearts have been so carefully protected by our unconscious armor. For some of us layers and layers and layers keep us safe and protect us from harm or pain or loss. The thing is that the protection doesn't work; all it does, in fact, is keeps us from feeling.

If you are in the midst of a heart break or grief, you have my compassion. First, feel that. My heart goes out to yours and touches it with the gentle embrace of knowing. Let the tears flow, let the anger burn, let the disappointment rattle your bones and then keep breathing. Take another breath and allow the feelings to flow. Allow the heart to break open even further.

Our hearts are not meant to be protected. Our hearts are designed to be brilliant, radiant, free, vulnerable and easily accessible. What has happened over the millennia, is the buildup of emotion not felt, resulting in packing one layer on top of another of that which you thought would keep you safe.

In *A Course in Miracles*, Lesson 153, it is said "In my defenselessness my safety lies."

Once the heart is freed from the layers of protection, it is free to Be, it is free to shine and to beat and nothing in all the world can change that. Yes, you might still be hurt and feel pain, but it will be a momentary pain and it will flow through. You might experience a sting and think: "Oh, that hurts," then breathe again and find love. Filling all the hollow places with love, cleansing and softening all the ragged and jagged edges with love brings a softness, a sweetness to your experience.

I was with a man recently in a heart opening workshop. He was filled with pain and grief as his long term relationship had just ended and not in a pretty way. He lost not only his girlfriend/partner but also her daughter whom he loved as well. You could see the pain in him. You could feel the distress. As we worked together it was as if his heart had to break even further. All he wanted was healing, but for that to happen, he had to allow all of his feelings to come out first, which felt like his heart had to break open even more.

When we experience heart break and grief, we open to the possibility of healing. I counsel anyone in grief, to allow it. Do not stop the feelings, and let the heart break wide open because then there is more room for love and grace and a deep healing.

Another man I worked with came to me filled with anger and bitterness, unforgiveness and pain in the betrayal and ending of his marriage. He came because it was eating him alive. He couldn't sleep or eat, he could hardly function. He was so caught up inside this cycle of distress he knew he had to shift out of it or it would kill him.

After our first Open Heart Meditation, he found peace for a moment, he found a breath's worth of relief. He was able to take a few deep breaths, perhaps the first he'd taken in months. He had made a pinpoint through his pain and anger and it was enough to begin. Over a few weeks, as he accessed a deeper part of his heart and a hint at what life might be like in the healing journey and beyond, he began to smile again, and to laugh. Over time, he came into full forgiveness, but not without processing and certainly not bypassing the pain. He has come to love even more fully than ever before, he found a new passion and purpose to his life and he lives with a wide open heart, trusting himself and that which is greater than him.

A woman I worked with came to me initially because she was in a big fat mess, emotionally, physically, logistically and legally even. She wanted me to fix the outer problems and help her feel better. What we worked on instead was accessing her higher heart. She had to dismantle her belief systems of being a victim, take responsibility for her role in her life situations and recognize the need to become true to her own heart. She had to release anger, fear and betrayal. She began to discover a new way of being that was less defensive and volatile and more gentle and true. She learned how to set boundaries without anger and to stand up for herself without fighting. She navigated through the various messes she came with and is today brilliantly bright, strong, self-sufficient and most of all happy with her life.

7

Sub-Layers of the Heart

The physical heart is an organ in your body that pumps the blood and keeps us alive on the planet. Without the heart and the heartbeat, we are dead. It is vital and central to our existence. Science is now telling us that the heart is the governing organ of the body and has its own brain. It is said that the heart has more neurons than the brain, yet we allow the brain to lead us, to forge our way. Consider this: when we access the heart we access a great and hidden power, one that is free from thought and belief; one that is aligned with a greater truth and awareness; one that knows Oneness and Wholeness. This heart has access not only to all of our own wisdom, but also to the wisdom of the universe. Let's head there now.

Deeper into the body lies the emotional heart. This is the seat of all emotions, the crossover place of feeling them. This is the place that gives us the polarity swings of, "Oh, I love you... Now, I hate you." It is meant to be a swinging door allowing all emotion to flow through without attachment or judgment. What has happened in our human experience is that the emotions get stuck and become habitual ways of being.

Think about how you live your life. Is there an emotion that is often present? One that sort of is the fabric of your being? If so, do you like it? Would you rather have something else as your foundation, perhaps love or joy or peace? Or even contentment or ease? There is a temptation for some people to get stuck at this layer of their hearts when doing heart work. But there is more... much, much more. There is a place that would compare the emotional heart to a neighborhood playground park with swings to Disney Land and all of its glory.

This is the land of the Spiritual Heart, which is deeper than the emotional heart. It is the heart of the universe - your higher, wiser heart. This is the heart that we will focus on. This heart is and was created to be the driving factor, it is the center of our bodies and the center of our souls. This heart is beyond physical, it is deep in our consciousness and is found behind and lower than the physical heart. Eastern traditions teach that there are many layers of the spiritual heart and that each layer takes us deeper and higher in consciousness.

The spiritual heart is the place of our divinity. It is where our infinite potential lies. It is the seed of the potential oak tree that is found within an acorn. It is sweet, rich, quiet and filled with possibilities. The experience of touching the spiritual heart is often one of bliss.

Accessing the spiritual heart is being so full you are empty or so empty that you are full. In its purity it is undefinable. It is the access point to creation, to the infinite. It is the doorway to the heavens. It is the crossover point between heaven and earth, between spiritual and physical, it is the point of creation itself creating through you.

It is pure unadulterated bliss. It blows the circuits of the mind and opens your soul to itself. When accessing this point, people often talk about the mystical experiences they have. This is true, however it is only the beginning, the very tip of an iceberg of possibilities.

Accessing the spiritual heart is possible to everyone always. In my workshops and events, people often land there and bask for a moment or two. Living from the spiritual heart is not only possible but is in fact what we are called to do. However, living there requires letting go of everything and anything that is unlike love.

The desire to live in and from the spiritual heart is the impulse to awaken. To awaken to the truth of who and what we are.

It is the yearning to come home, to access the point of knowing Oneness and experiencing Wholeness. The process is to touch the heart space again and again, each time perhaps for longer moments at a time.

The spiritual heart is likened to the quantum field. It is accessible and experience-able. However, it cannot be thought into. You cannot think your way there and there is no thought in that place. You may receive a hit or hint of inspiration, but you won't be thinking about it. Once you think about it, you have left the field.

Touching the field, diving deep into it, basking there begins to build new neuro-pathways, new thought pathways and ultimately develops into the habitual way of being.

For now, wherever you are along your path - touch your heart space as often as possible. Learn to land in your heart and lead from your heart. There are many variations, many hues, many subtle distinctions within the spiritual heart and at this point, they don't matter too much.

When we learn to access and live from our hearts, life changes. The decisions you make might be different and certainly the intentions behind the decisions will be. Your basis will be love and Oneness, rather than separation and fear. Drop into your heart on a regular basis and begin to build this new muscle.

Let's take a moment to do that now: *Close your eyes and take a deep breath in. As you exhale, relax. Focus for a few breaths on breathing deeply and fully exhaling. Become aware of your body. Feel your head and notice the backs of your eyes. Feel your feet firmly on the ground. Open your palms and become aware of them. Bring your awareness from the top of your head to your feet. Draw your awareness up through your legs, hips and torso, landing in your heart area. If you can't find your heart, drop again down into your hips and rest there for a moment.*

Bringing your awareness up from your hips to your heart, feel it. Imagine seeing it, as the physical organ that it is, pumping blood, supporting life in your body. Imagine dropping into the center of your heart, finding yourself in a cave of exquisite crystalline light. Feel the safety, the support, the security of being in the safe place deep in your heart.

From the deeper heart, you can bask. You can rest. Here you are filled with light, love, energy and inspiration. Rest quietly here until you feel an impulse coming from the depths of your being. You are supported, you are loved.

Feel the love that is. The love that is for you, with you, as and in you. Feel the love that penetrates and permeates your being. Let this love overflow your heart and enfold your entire being. How much more love can you receive? Receive it and then a bit more.

When you are ready, feel this love moving throughout your body, into your feet, grounding it through your being. Feel it moving through your hands and head. Anchor the experience and bring it forward, back into this present moment. Gently open your eyes. And so it is.

8

Creating Space

One of my super powers is that of creating and holding space. Why is that a superpower? In this day and age, how many of us are stressed for time? We live stressed and all tied up over something or someone. We worry, we fret, we are anxious and we don't even remember that peace is possible, much less seek it. We think that what we see on the news defines our lives. We think that the weather or stock market can affect us.

We fill our minds with the media images of violence, murder, tragic accidents, off-the-wall political decrees and words of warning about so many things that could harm us, make us afraid or be cause for worry.

The result is a physiological stress on our systems. We physically get tied up in knots, we physically block the flow with obstructions. Picture a big beautiful skein of yard, as it is purchased. It is perfect in the way the strands weave around and around each other. There is order in the skein that allows for flow. When you pull the strand, it moves smoothly and if no one messes with it, it will continue all the way to the end.

But see the order in this unraveling. The yarn gets tangled at some point and there is struggle and suffering. In our lives, when we are touched by something that causes us to feel fear or anger, frustration or the unknown, we contract, or tighten up. With the yarn if we pull it, it gets knotted up. The more we try to pull on it, the tighter the knot gets and the more tangled the mess becomes.

It is the same with us. Imagine we are that skein of yarn. We have energy systems that are wound around each other in perfect order. There is spaciousness and order to it, there is room to flow and use what is necessary (like the yarn being pulled out for use). Then something happens, usually triggering an emotion of some sort. It could be watching the news or checking your bank account balance. It could be a life challenge for yourself or a loved one, a health issue, or relationship bump. It can be anything; a close call avoiding an incident or a terrible accident, a cross word from a boss or a stranger, or anything in between.

It doesn't matter what the cause is, the result is a tightening up, a contraction in the system. When contraction happens the natural response is to pull in further, thereby tightening and constricting the system even more.

Visualize your perfect skein of yarn getting tangled up into a big tight mess. Unknowingly, as we try to get out of it, we actually pull it tighter and tighter resulting in a big knot. It looks and feels impossible to get through. There is temptation to cut into the middle of it and unravel the knot that way, but you know that won't really work. So what to do?

Create space or spaciousness. Picture a knotted ball of yarn. There appears to be no order nor any solution, but being determined, you begin to work it. The first thing you have to do is create a little space around it. I think of getting a knot in my gold chain. I have to be very careful as I handle it, that the knot does not get tighter, or the chain breaks. I instead have to manipulate it gently, easily to loosen it. I do that by creating space and the result is a spaciousness. Once there is space in the midst of the knot, the way through becomes apparent. It might still take a few tries, further unraveling and creating space, but you will find the way.

It is the same with our emotional knots. Think of, imagine or feel an emotional knot. I realize it's a bit harder if there is not an active one, but call to your awareness a recent emotional moment. Perhaps it was a little bump in your road, or perhaps it was that one big, huge one that you think you have handled over and over again in your life, that just peeks its gnarly head up once in a while to remind you it's still there.

Let's take that one. Identify it. Activate the feelings around it, let it begin to come alive in your system and awareness. Let the feeling build so you are feeling it in your body, not just thinking about it. This is very important. Find it, and bring it forward. Many of these hidden patterns like to stay just under the surface, so they impact you, but are not totally conscious. As we begin to create space for them, as we begin to allow them to simply be without any story about it, they actually can breathe themselves. As they are breathing, and you are creating a safe space for them to be felt and expressed, they begin to lose their power over you.

Creating space is as simple as allowing. Creating space is like becoming a witness to that which is inside of you. It is free of judgment and resistance. It is simply energy running. Think of a big beach ball that you are trying to keep under the water. You know the game. The harder you try to keep it down, the higher it jumps up when you lose control over it. The beach ball is not designed to be under the water and the more you try to keep it there, the more power it has in its release. It often will burst out at totally inappropriate times and ways. It will create a huge splash and douse you with the impact.

At the pool, it's funny. In our emotional lives, it can be destructive. Creating space for the beach ball to rest on the surface of the water is quieter than trying to keep it below the surface. The beach ball is designed to float on the surface. When you allow the beach ball to be what it is and not try to control it or make it be something else entirely, it is innocuous. It has no power over you, it is not bad or wrong, it is only a beach ball. Something to play with, to get some enjoyment out of or leave it alone, either way, it doesn't matter. When we allow our emotions to flow through, they simply are. When we fight them or try to keep them down below the surface, they also can pop up in destructive ways, dousing you and others around you with a huge spray of aftermath.

Creating space not only allows for the tight spaces in our lives to be loosened, it allows life to flow more beautifully.

Recently I was working with a group of women, asking them what their hearts desired. Overwhelmingly, the consistent answer was time and space to simply be. We need time and space to rest, revitalize, to remember and nurture our souls, to unravel the stuff of life and come back to ourselves, to breathe and think and connect. We need the time and space for our souls to catch up with our bodies.

Creating space in our emotions creates spaces in our minds, which in turn creates space in our lives. Time and space are gifts that we often don't give ourselves. Give yourself a gift: create some space today! Clear off a counter, empty a drawer, straighten up a room, then sit for an allotted amount of time with a cup of tea. Create space to be.

The Truth About Surrender

Creating space is really about surrendering. Surrendering is the letting go of all resistance to what is. The word surrender has taken a lot of heat over the years. It brings up an image of a weak and wimpy doormat or of completely giving up after a long battle. Sometimes, surrender implies a very painful and traumatic process of letting go of what you don't want to let go of, like ripping Velcro apart very slowly.

Surrender, in the purest sense of the word, is quite different. It is sweet. There's a song we used to sing - Sweet Surrender. *I'm opening up to sweet surrender to the luminous love light of the one. I'm opening, I'm opening*. How sweet is that? As I'm in memory of singing that song years and years ago. I wonder why it didn't occur to me when I was in the throes of battle with my own surrender?

Surrender in its purest form is relaxing. Simply relax. You know how to do that, or maybe you don't. I was talking with my friend just the other day and she told me how tied up she was, that she couldn't just relax. I said well just relax. She said, "I can't. I don't know how; I'm too tied up."

Relax. Right Now! This one thing could be the key to a life of greater ease.

Drop your shoulders. Feel your feet on the ground. Breathe in deeply and feel the air entering through your nose and moving down into your body. Feel your lungs and belly expand and release.

Relaxing is like exhaling. Simply let the air go. There is nothing you have to do but let go. Unfurl your fists, unclench your jaw, stretch your neck. Breathe again. Notice the breath entering your body and feel it exiting.

Imagine that all your stress could be released as simply as exhaling. Sit down right now and do this. *Take a deep breath in and hold it for a moment. Then let it go. Exhale, all the way, push the air out of your system and feel the space being made for new, fresh air. Inhale, hold and exhale, this time consciously letting the stress that might be in your body or mind release. Feel it falling off your body and going into the ground. With each breath, let more stress release. Feel your shoulders dropping, your chest expanding, your neck and shoulders relaxing. What else do you notice? What happens to your jaw, your palms? Do your arms and legs get heavy? How is your brain? More open? A little less tied up?*

9

Believe it Because We See it? Or See it Because We Believe it?

Tina Turner has a song entitled, *What's Love Got to Do with It*? I'm posing a question, "What's Belief Got to Do with it?" Or to ask it another way, why do you believe what you believe?

"Whatever the mind can conceive and believe, it can achieve." — Napoleon Hill
Think and Grow Rich.

What is belief? Google tells us that belief is an acceptance that a statement is true or that something exists, as in "his belief in the value of hard work".

But why do you believe what you believe? Who taught you that? Is it True for you? Does it matter? We believe lots of things every day that may or may not be true. Let's unpack a few of the beliefs we have that simply are NOT true.

- I'm unworthy
- I'm not lovable
- I'm wrong
- I'm broken
- The system sucks
- Life is hard

- If I work hard, I'll make it
- My financial success defines me
- I am my body
- My family defines me
- We are doomed on this planet
- Add a few of your own beliefs here...

Here are few other beliefs - try them on for size. Do you believe them?

- I am worthy
- I am a success
- I love, I am loved, I am lovable
- I can do anything I want
- I love money and money loves me
- I am One with all that is and infinite possibilities
- I am a child of God in whom God is well pleased
- I have free choice to do with my life as I desire
- I can have all that I want and more
- I create my life
- Life is good and meant to be fun and abundant and filled with joy
- Add a few more here...

Which beliefs are expansive? Which are contractive? If you really could choose your beliefs, which would you choose? Why don't you?

Our belief system was primarily handed down to us by our parents, ancestors and culture. Most of them are not questioned, they are simply input into our subconscious and once there, they become the foundation of our lives, through which all things pass. What if we could extract the beliefs that no longer serve us and replace them with new, expansive and supportive beliefs? We can. It is possible. When you extract and dissolve limiting beliefs and replace them with expansive supportive beliefs, your life can take on a whole new experience.

There are three ways to change our beliefs and to change our consciousness. One is through emotional trauma, which in most cases, involves suffering. Change can come through repetition, doing something different again and again, so that the patterns change and suffering ends. The third is what we call a quantum shift. It is the basis and foundation of this book. Let's take a look at each of the methods, but first identify with a belief that you have that you'd like to explore.

For example, let's play with the belief that life is a struggle. First, do you believe it? How does this belief show up in your life? What are the patterns and indicators that you believe it? If you didn't, what might you believe instead? Let's explore a few ways to change a belief.

Emotional impact can change a belief. It often comes as a trauma, drama or other such challenging situation. Perhaps a life-threatening diagnosis for yourself or a loved one, sometimes an accident, or loss of a job or loved one. Anything that is traumatic has the potential to uproot and unravel a belief system. This is not my preferred method, but I have walked it a few times. It is jarring in such a way that old structures crumble.

When life happens in such a way, we come into question and the questioning can lead to new ways of thinking and believing. An emotional impact that might change the belief "life is a struggle," might be one that causes you to change your perspective and values. You might be shaken up in a way that causes a new thought like "I'm going to enjoy every moment" to replace the old belief. Usually these are reactions and not conscious decisions.

Repetition of a statement can eventually change belief. Repetition can also be known as affirmations. Affirmations are statements of truth repeated until you begin to believe them. One of my favorite, long-time, very popular affirmations used with repetition was presented by Rev. Stretton Smith in his *4-T Prosperity Program*. It was a 12-week program taught in many new thought churches. The first week assignment that continued through the 12 weeks was to affirm, "I am prosperous" 100 times a day.

This worked for many people and is still used today. However, if, when affirming I am prosperous, your belief system is something like money is bad, or I don't have enough, those statements/beliefs will override your affirmation.

To use repetition, activate the frequency of that which is being affirmed. I am prosperous. Feel it, activate it and clear anything and everything that is unlike it. I am prosperous. Feel it, explore it, what does that even mean? Define it and play with it over time. What you are doing now is aligning your frequency to that which you desire. Now if you have a conflicting thought, you can deal with it by looking, seeing, allowing and changing the thought pattern.

Repetition eventually changes the subconscious, replacing an old belief with a new one as you believe it. Repetition can change a belief when added with frequency.

My friend and colleague, Rev. Mary Morrissey teaches in her *Dream Builder* and *Prosperity Plus* courses about changing the TV channel. Perhaps you are constantly tuned to the CNN (constantly negative news) Channel. What if now you become more interested in the Adventure or Travel channels? Every time you notice that you are tuned to CNN, change the channel. Become more interested in the Adventure or Travel channels.

Repetition in this manner, will eventually instill a new belief that replaces the old, just like the new channel replaces CNN. Over time, the automatic response will shift from the CNN channel to the channel of choice. To change "life is a struggle," we might use something like, "I love my life. I take each moment and opportunity as a growth possibility." This method takes time and consistency. We will discover in a later chapter, **Accessing the Subconscious,** a quick, simple and easy method of changing beliefs by accessing the subconscious mind directly.

10

A Look at Fear

In this world today, so many people live in fear in varying degrees. Fear is an interesting phenomenon. It pulls people together and it tears them apart. It is used by some in authority or power positions as a weapon to control the people. It so often results in violence, which in turn generates more fear.

Fear can be a vicious cycle, it is insidious and contagious. What is the antidote to fear? Love. Oneness. Knowing or finding that which is greater than the illusion. A little disclaimer here - fear as I'm using it here is the emotional and psychological fear that permeates and penetrates the consciousness of our world at this time. I'm not talking about the fear that takes place when you come face to face with a literal and physical bear. That is an entirely different emotion and does different things in our body chemistry. It also ends, one way or another. I'm talking about the culture of living in fear day after day after day.

Fear is insidious, it's sneaky and it's there to keep you safe, which often means, small and unfulfilled. Take a look at the following list and see if there is anything that gets bumped up in you or around you. There is no right or wrong answer. In fact, feel the fear right now of a test coming on. Will I pass it? What if I guess wrong? What will happen???

Feel into these scenarios:

- Coming across an angry person in a store
- Facing a gun
- Sitting next to people who don't look like you
- Checking your bank account and finding out that there is no money left at the end of the month
- Standing on a cliff about to jump off on a zip line tether
- Taking off by yourself on a journey across the country
- Needing to tell someone you love something they don't want to hear
- Standing up to your boss
- Hearing strange noises outside your home in the dark
- The electricity going out and the storms coming
- The thought of losing everything material that you own
- Driving in a city you don't know
- Traveling abroad to country you are uncomfortable in
- Traveling to a country that scares you
- Watching scary movies
- Taking a leap of faith in a new career direction
- Sending your child off by themselves for the first time
- Watching your son race motorcycles, really fast
- Hearing or receiving a serious diagnosis for yourself or a loved one
- Watching a neighbor, who sucks your energy dry, come to your door,

- Hearing a particular voice in your head telling you to watch out
- What else activates fear in you?

As you read through that list, notice what gets triggered and what comes up. Do you rationalize and believe that some places you should have fear? What is your relationship with the idea of fear right now? There are no right or wrong answers, just awareness.

Fear, as we know it, is a layer of energy that actually prevents you from accessing your true self. Fear can be utilized as a catalyst for more life, but most often it drains us and stops us from being present in the moment.

Fear has been defined as: **F**alse **E**vidence **A**ppearing **R**eal, or a **F**requency of **E**nergy **A**ltering our **R**eality.
Consider this. Fear is simply an emotion and emotions are energy in motion. When fear appears, what if you could allow it. Feel it and let it move through your awareness without resistance. Remember:

Resistance to what is, causes suffering.

Feel the fear and do it anyway. I'm picturing high divers, up on the platform getting ready to dive or jump off. They do just it. Feel the fear and do it anyway. Feel the fear of public speaking, and do it anyway. Feel the fear that moves, notice it without judgment and let it flow through you. Sometimes, it might trigger a deeper layer, but most often, especially as you practice this, it will move right along. Listen to it, watch it as an observer. Notice how it lands in your body and where it gets stuck. Become aware of it and let it be.

What would it be like to be open to the possibility of life without fear? Some might say you would become careless. I don't think so. Some would say, "you won't be safe," but is that true based on our discussion here? Does fear equate with safety?

What could you do if you knew that you could not fail? Jana Stanfield has a beautiful song about that called *"If I Were Brave"*. What would you do if you were brave? How does being brave compare with fear? What would I do today if I were brave and open to the possibility of life without fear dictating your action? In the face of fear, you can take an attitude of "what do I choose to do?" If you did that, what would you be like? Would you be more empowered or less?

Fear does not keep you safe - just in case you were still wondering. Fear, in fact, does the opposite. Wisdom keeps you safe. Fear is that which causes you to either flee, fight or freeze. Fear is an energy vibration that draws to it, that which it is. That which we vibrate to, is what we attract.

Someone once said:

It is not what we want that we attract;
it is what we are that attracts.

If you are filled with a sense of fear and worry, it makes your vibrational field fuzzy and thick. The vibrational field is the energy that you are both standing in and emanating, that which becomes the attractive quality and sets the tone for what you will see and receive. When we can raise our vibration into peace, love or joy, the field is rich and ready for the harvest.

Can you see this? Fear muddies up the waters of life. Fear plugs, obstructs and blocks the flow of Life. It is the flow of life that we are seeking, for in that comes all we desire. In the flow we are free. In the flow we are able to see and co-create with clarity.

Imagine this: You are standing on the banks of a great river. Along the edges the water is choppy, it is filled with debris, rocks, sticks, an undergrowth that is hard to navigate. This is life as we know it. But take a look out in to the center of the river. Here the waters flow along smoothly. Here there are no obstructions, here it is peaceful and relaxing. The work is to get from the banks of the river, observing your life happening to you, through the muck and gunk of the outer edges into the Center, into the Flow, into the place of ease and grace. In the center of the river, there is a raft. When you are able to get onto that raft, you can relax and bask, as long as you allow the current to take you. Do not get onto the raft and then try paddling upstream. It won't work, it will exhaust you and it's just not really where you want to go anyway.

Fear is the muck and gunk of the edges of the river bank. Move through your fear, turn and face it, feel it - do not try to stop it or make it go away. Fear is an emotion that needs to be acknowledged and allowed. As you do that, you can breathe through it and it will begin to dissipate.

Now, you might be saying, I don't have fear. I understand. I said that too. I never lived in an awareness of fear. I was sort of fear-less, people often talked of my courage in the choices I made and actions I took. It wasn't until many years later that I realized how deeply fear had its grip into me. For me, it showed up in not wanting to hurt another person's feeling, it came disguised as wanting to do what was right and wrapped up in a blanket of caring what I thought other people thought I should be thinking.

Do you see that in yourself? It's not fear, or is it? I was such a good girl, in part because I feared conflict. I followed my heart and my own drummer in many areas of my life, but in others, I lived for that illusive idea of what I thought others thought I should think.

The thing about fear is that it only works when it is hidden. What I mean by that is fear lives and feeds in the dark. Remember the movie, *Monsters, Inc.?* The monsters hid in the closets and when it was dark, they jumped out and scared the little children. Most of them hid and screamed. But one little girl, laughed. Her laughter broke all sense of fear. It took the monsters by surprise and they did not know how to act. Fear breeds in the dark and the unknown.

Bring the fear from the dark to the light
and it loses its power.

Relax into Fear Exercise: *Feel the fear and do it anyway. In the moment that we fully feel our fear, we are freed from it. We can begin to embody a greater point of attraction. Relax into the resistance. Relax and begin to welcome the fear. Relax your body. Relax your mind. Imagine you are letting go of the grip you have on fear, and it is being freed from you to go about its merry way. Imagine that it slides right off of you, as you relax. Discover it was you holding it, not it holding you. Begin to cultivate a welcoming of fear. When you can be with it, you no longer have to resist it, buy in to it, try to change it or have it be different. Be with the fear you feel. Relax even more deeply now. Who would you be without fear? Be that person. What would you do without the fear holding you back? Do that thing.*

11

One Key to End Suffering for All Time

You have come to remember who you are in Wholeness and Oneness. Suffering comes from our belief in separation. Here is one key to end all suffering through separation - know that it is an illusion - a big one - one that has the wool pulled over all of our faces. Now, that is not a bad thing, we've lived with the illusion for a very, very long time. Once upon a time in the beginning of humankind, we decided to come to know ourselves as separate. It was a game; it was an experiment. It was, in the beginning like playing a blind-fold game.

Someone, as in the collective, liked it, we liked the power that seemed to come from being alone. It was new and different. The availability of this experience was vast. In the illusion of separation, we came to believe we were invincible, powerful and independent. Now it is time to realize that separation is an illusion and that in fact we are all connected as one humanity, all sharing this grand planet earth. We are as individual as the organs in our body, yet we are all one body, one humankind. When we realize this, all suffering will end and peace will emerge.

What is the one thing that keeps you from peace?

Peace is Only A Blink Away

In fact, peace is found right here and right now. Peace is a quality and state of being from the inside out. As I write this, there are hundreds of people, including my friend, Bob, who are demonstrating on the capital lawn for reform in the political system. It is the Democracy Spring Rally and is being held in April 2016. Yesterday there were over 800 protestors standing quietly, and not so quietly, but calmly on the lawn to protest government corruption and money in politics. There were thousands of people arrested. Bob was charged with "crowding" and "*incommodating*," which we don't even know what that means. The next day, his wife, Noel, was arrested with about 80 others standing together.

The week before, I had a conversation with Bob and Noel on their Co-Creator's Convergence call. It was entitled: *Does Conscious Co-Creation Really Work*. The premise of our conversation is that we live in two different dimensions at the same time. One is wholeness the other separation. We are usually only aware of the state of separation for this is the consciousness of the planet at this time. However, there is at the same time, a different dimension, a consciousness of wholeness, even if we are not conscious of it. This is the place of our divinity. This is the very real place of our Essence and higher self. This is what we are waking up to. The place of wholeness is our spiritual truth. It is the absolute truth, whereas the experience of separation is part of our illusion/illusory world.

The world of illusion is just that, illusion or appearances. We, as humanity, have been so trained and so vested in the illusion that we see no other possibility. When we awaken, we begin to see differently, we begin to experience life differently.

So, you see there is great risk in awakening. The systems that are in place will crumble - not from some outside force, but from the ground. As we awaken, we will not only no longer tolerate greed and corruption, but we won't even be able to see it. When that happens, corruption crumbles.

Does that mean we get to bury our heads in the sand with spiritual platitudes? No, but it does mean that we can do peaceful protests from two places. *[See Resources for a link to listen to the conversation we had with Bob and Noel on the program.]* Let's play out the polarities of possibility.

One possibility is that we join into the rally which is initially planned as a peaceful protest and we very quickly get caught up into the emotion. And there are lots and lots of emotions. Think for a moment about the rallies led by either Martin Luther King or Gandhi. They were about non-violence and peace, and they were very emotional.

Being caught in the emotion leads to a certain outcome. Tempers rise, voices get louder, people get more and more crazed about both the possibility and the "wrong" that they are protesting. Can you feel it in your body right now? Go ahead, let it rip. Feel into injustice. Feel into anger and a sense of "it's just wrong, and I'm not going to stand for it anymore!" Feel into anytime you've been violated and taken advantage of. Feel the emotions and let yourself get caught up in the energy and flow. It is in this place that most of us go and hang out. Either that, or we stay away and ignore the issues and bury our heads in the sand, sometimes saying things like “Spirit is in charge, it’s all in divine order.”

Take a deep breath and let that go. For the paradox, for the experience, now imagine standing in the center of a beautiful field. You are whole, peaceful, and peace filled. You are love embodied and relaxed. In this place, you are. In this place, we call it the field, but it is also the place of wholeness, of oneness, of your soul beyond this physical life of separation. This place is accessible, and we’ll tackle that a bit later. For now, let perfect peace permeate, penetrate and fill your awareness. Let it touch all the places that are hard and rigid, that are righteous and angry. Let it soften you for only a moment.

Bask here. Stay here until your body relaxes, your soul responds and your mind is quiet. Look around the field, and see only peace. Feel only peace and contentment and connection.

Connection is a key here, take a few more breaths and let connection permeate, penetrate and fill the interspaces of your being. Relax a bit more. Relax and let go deeper and deeper.

Stand tall and look around your field to the edges. Imagine the peace rally and all that it means to you. Imagine being in this state of peace and connection as you enter into the rally. Your peace, your authenticity, your connection overrides your emotions. Stand here in the midst of the rally. Stand here in the midst of the noise, the chanting, the crowds. Stand here in the midst of seeing your friends being arrested. You are making a difference.

Your connection is changing the energy of the event. You might not see it or feel it right away and you might get caught up into the emotions. No worries either way. When you remember, go once again to the field of connection, to the possibility that this very thing is what will tip the scale. Take a split second to remember that in Truth there is peace in the midst. There is love at the core. There will come a time where peace and love prevail. Why not now, why not you?

When we are able to stand in peace and a conscious connection, we hold a very different energy and vibration. When we forget and get caught up into injustice, intolerance, anger, guilt and frustration, we are pushed off our centers.

Again, no worries, just stand up again and return to your center. And again and again. Return to peace and love as often as you can remember. Each time we are making an impact and a difference in the collective consciousness. It's not that we don't feel those powerful emotions, it's that we aren't run by them, dominated by them. When we acknowledge them and act from our center, the actions have a different and more effective outcome.

12

A Word About Emotions

Emotions are real and they need to be acknowledged, accepted and allowed. Emotions, however are not the truth of who we are. They are simply something that we have and that we get to experience.

Emotions are energy in motion (e-motion).

When our emotions are allowed, felt and experienced fully, they bring to us freedom. When a young toddler is mad and cries her heart out there comes a moment when it is done, complete. She then immediately moves on to the next thing, gets up and goes to play. In the completion of feeling and expressing the emotions, comes a quiet freedom. Feeling emotions fully, however, does not give us permission to act badly, nor is it for the weak of heart.

For example, when we are angry, and I mean really, really angry, like in a rage against something, acknowledging the anger, accepting that it is there and allowing it to flow or burn through you, creates energy that can be used in productive, proactive ways. Allowing anger does not give us license to scream or destruct or use violence. Feeling it and allowing it can all be done in consciousness.

I know there is something that makes you angry, that gets your rage up and flowing. Bring it into your awareness now and let it begin to build. Where do you feel it in your body? What does it feel like? Does it burn? Like a raging fire or a pile of embers? If the anger that you are feeling had a shape to it, what shape would it be? What color? Feel it accumulating, feel it building. Then feel it fully. Your body might shake; it might feel like its burning up inside. Feel it. Allow it. Scream into a pillow, beat a bed if you have to, but let it begin to be freed from your cells.

Anger in itself is not bad, it simply is. To release the emotional tension around anger, keep feeling it and begin to gather it. Gather the anger and let it exit your body, being collected in a container. You might imagine a huge barrel in front of you that can gather the anger. Spend the time here, let it work through you and fill the container. When it feels time, go to the container and begin to lift it up. It might be very heavy at first, lift it anyway. Lift it hip level, then chest level. Do you notice that it is getting lighter? Lift it up to eye level and on a count of three toss it up into the sky. As you do this, the anger dissipates and disappears. What is left is pure possibilities.

Take a moment to allow a new energy to be poured into you, replacing and filling the spaces that anger had held. It could be light, love, warmth or peace; allow it to be whatever it is. Take another moment to allow a new idea to be birthed in you. Perhaps it is an action you can take. Let the thing that the anger was about be looked at without the emotion. Let it lead you to a new way of being. Do something with it. Acknowledge it and feel the power. Anger is always an indicator of a boundary being pushed up against.

The trick is that the emotion of anger gets us sidetracked. When we free the emotionality of it, we are empowered to take action. It is quite fascinating and freeing. Now breathe some more. Come back to center and let the residual dissipate. Begin to integrate the new energy through your body, mind and soul. Notice what you notice and if you can, spend a bit of time writing about this experience and idea.

Peace is possible. Peace is a state of consciousness that can be found in the midst of every situation and every moment. Peace is the calm at the eye of the storm. In the storm, especially the tornadoes and hurricanes, there is a space in the center where everything is calm and quiet. You can access this anytime you choose. You can even be in the field of peace in the midst of being angry. You cannot however, take baby steps into peace, you cannot take baby steps into calm. It is a different layer of consciousness. You have to leap or drop into it.

Let's look at it another way. When you are in the throes of anger or any other emotion, it is nearly impossible to move out of it, isn't it? It is like pulling a huge burden through a thick forest and into the meadow. It is not the best use of energy or time. However, if you can notice that you have anger, that you are in the throes of it, then you can take a breath. Notice it, allow it, feel it for a moment. This isn't about making it go away or ignoring it or denying it. It is acknowledging it, accepting and allowing it. In the accepting and allowing there comes a choice point. You can choose. Say to yourself, "I am so angry that it's burning in and through me. And I'm going to feel it all the way through. I'm going to let it burn until I can drop into the field. I'm going to let it burn in a way that gathers it so I can release it and experience relief." This will take varying amounts of time and consciousness. Then choose again. "Oh, I'm having anger. Cool. Let it burn." Then find yourself in the field and let it gather. When it feels like time, begin to lift the container like we did before.

You cannot lift the container of your anger, or other emotion without acknowledging, accepting and allowing it to be what it is. As you lift it, you can drop back into the field. As you lift it, it becomes transcended into love, light, grace or peace. As the emotion is lifted, the space that is created is empty for a moment. It can easily be filled with love or another positive vibration. Allow a new belief to be revealed to consciously fill the space. Nature abhors a vacuum. As anger is lifted, transcend it and replace it with a Truth statement like: I am filled with peace. I am peace-filled. I am at peace. Let the new vibration then permeate, penetrate and fill the interspaces of your consciousness and being.

13

Finding the Elusive Peace That You Desire and Deserve

Peace is what we seek. Peace is what feels elusive. Peace in our hearts and lives, peace in our family and relationships, peace in the world. Is that too much to ask for? Apparently, it might be. The thing is that we seek the peace outside of us and we will never find it there. We often want peace on the outer so we can feel peace on the inner. That, my friend is backwards. First and foremost, peace is a state of being. Peace is available in the midst of each and every moment. It does not depend on or require any situation or circumstance to be discovered. And discovered is a good descriptive word for experiencing peace, like discovering a beautiful jewel or hidden treasure.

Let's define it. Peace is the absence of suffering and struggle; it is freedom from disturbance; it is, quiet and tranquility. Peace is an energy of smooth, clear waters. Peace is quiet and passive. Peace is alive, active and vibrant. Peace is a state of mind that is allowing and accepting of all things.

Peace and Ease

What we seek is peace. Or is it? Think about your struggles and your suffering. In the depths of those, are you seeking peace? Or is it too far away in those moments? Perhaps what we are really seeking is ease. Ease defined is the absence of difficulty or effort.

Ease is easier to reach, for peace appears to be elusive at times, but we can always reach ease. Ease can be found in chunks. From wherever you are, it can be a bit easier, if only microscopically. Peace either is or it isn't being experienced. You can't be "sort of" peaceful. You can't be sort of pregnant. You are or you aren't. Ease gives us more flavors and choices. Ease gives us a spectrum, and provides stepping stones from the depths of emotion to peace. I believe that ease is any relief. How could this moment be any easier? It is more reachable, more easily attainable.

Even in the midst of suffering and struggle, you can find ease. It is there, like a life-line, if only we can become aware of it. In the awareness, ease appears. Can this be easier?

EASE as an acronym is:

Effortless

Awareness of

Spirit and

Excellence

14

Would it be Alright with You if Life Got Easier?

When I first heard these words in 1999 from a teacher of mine, Maria Nemeth, it floored me. It woke me up to a new possibility. I couldn't even fathom that life could be easier! I had moments when life flowed beautifully and although I wasn't living that all the time, I had experienced it. I knew moments when life was down right rough and tough. I recalled scriptures that were the basis for all that I did, my credo, if you will.

- Matt 19:26 - With God all things are possible.
- John 14:12 - Very truly I tell you, whoever believes in me will do the works I have been doing, and they will do even greater things than these, because I am going to the Father.
- John 15:11 - I have told you this so that my joy may be in you and that your joy may be complete.
- John 16:24 - Ask and you will receive, and your joy will be complete.
- John 10:10 - I am come that they may have life, and may have it more abundantly.

I realized that I still had a sense deep within me that I had to work hard, that I had to sacrifice in order to be good, that life had a certain struggle built into it.

What I discovered over time is that life does have a certain level of struggle built into it. Part of the struggle is our identification with the illusion of separation. We've been talking about that throughout this book. The other part of struggle built into life is the struggle to be born or birthed, the struggle for the bird to hatch from the egg, the butterfly to emerge from the chrysalis.These struggles are actually muscle builders and are necessary for life. Now I reframe even those struggles. The struggles that are life building muscles do not carry the same emotional suffering as does the struggle in separation. In the struggle of life, of being born there is a beautiful sense of purpose in the struggle.

Think about a goal you might have. Perhaps it is to run a marathon. When you make the decision to run a marathon (insert your own goal here, build a business, eat healthier, make more money, change how you are in relationship to someone, etc.), there is first a commitment. In the commitment lies all that you need to reach and complete it.

"Until one is committed, there is hesitancy, the chance to draw back, always ineffectiveness. Concerning all acts of initiative (and creation), there is one elementary truth that ignorance of which kills countless ideas and splendid plans: that the moment one definitely commits oneself, then Providence moves too. All sorts of things occur to help one that would never otherwise have occurred. A whole stream of events issues from the decision, raising in one's favor all manner of unforeseen incidents and

meetings and material assistance, which no man could have dreamed would have come his way. Whatever you can do, or dream you can do, begin it. Boldness has genius, power, and magic in it. Begin it now."

-Goethe

In the commitment comes a decision. The decision to do whatever it takes to get it done. The decision to set daily/ weekly intentions and meet them. The goals will increase with time. The first day you might walk ¼ mile and call it good. The next day 2 miles. Systematically, moving in the direction of your dreams, endeavoring to live into your dream or goal, you will progress, you will begin to build muscle, habits and patterns that support your growth and stamina. As you move into running for longer periods, there will be a certain stretching that happens--a stretching of your endurance, your muscles and your rhythm. At the end of a run, when your body is screaming and you are exhausted, sweating and wanting to drop, you can still feel good about the effort. Some call that suffering and struggle. It might be, but now we can also see that struggle of building muscle is for a greater good.

"If one advances confidently in the direction of his dreams, and endeavors to live the life which he has imagined, he will meet with a success unexpected in common hours".

- Henry David Thoreau

15

The Great Grand Vision

When there is a greater goal, a vision to hold onto, the daily tasks or steps become easier to tackle; they become more meaningful in the context of the dream.

I have a grand vision for my life. It's beautiful, brilliant and it lifts me up when I am believing in it! Oh yes! Absolutely. This is it! I can do this! I am empowered, energized and expanded in my vision. It comes to me from on high, it appears and lands into my awareness rather than me creating it in my mind. I love it. I get chills when I feel into it. It's so amazing, it is my soul's work, it is my gift and contribution to the world. It's just awesome.

Then my head can get ahold of this vision and work with it. Sometimes it goes like this, (you might relate): It's awesome! I'm alive with possibilities. Oh, well, maybe it's pretty cool. It's an ok dream, but you know you don't really want to work that hard and that long for this. It would be ok if I didn't have this dream. Then I wouldn't get disappointed if I didn't reach it. Oh, so really, I could do this instead. That fits better into who I think I am, I wouldn't have to stretch so much or work so hard. Yea, that would be alright...

Can you feel the energy drain and downward spiral as I move from what my soul longs for to a much smaller dream? Something my personality thinks might be achievable? I just went from having a dream to run a marathon to deciding to walk around my block.

Now there is absolutely nothing wrong with wanting to walk around your block, even as a dream or vision, if it is real. However, in my decades of working with people, I found that most of us have hidden dreams that scare the bejeezus out of us. Those are the ones I'm talking about. Those are the ones that will push and pull you from who you think you are right now into who you are becoming, the greatest, grandest version of yourself.

Let's play. *Exercises to Stretch our goal muscles.*

- If there were no limits in your life, what would you love, love, love to be doing?
- If you had no worries about what others thought of you, what would you love?
- If money were no issue...
- If you had no voices in your head that said things like.... - You can't, you shouldn't, you won't...
- If you had only voices that said... You go Girl! You go guy! You can do this...
- If time was no issue... what would you love? Where would you live? What would you do?
- If you had no other obligations to care for others, family, kids, parents, spouses, etc... what then?
- If you were writing the script of your life, in the dreamiest, grandest, movie, what would your life look like in 10 years? 20? 5?

- If you were totally and completely fulfilled and content, what would you tell someone else who is stuck in "life as we know it?"

Call out all of the reasons why you haven't achieved this yet. List out all of your excuses. Keep going until you have 20 excuses or reasons listed. List them especially if you think you shouldn't be saying that.

Drop into your heart and feel into the dream again, as if it is already achieved. How would you feel? What would you be doing differently than you are now? What would you be saying? Where would you be spending your time? Who did you need to become, what did you need to embody in order to achieve this dream?

Final step - list out two or three simple, concrete action steps that you can take today to begin to put the vibration of this dream into place in your life right now. If you want to run a marathon, go buy some good shoes. If you want to travel the world, go to a travel agent and get brochures. Simple, easy things that you can do to let yourself know you are serious about this and committed to it!

What do you have to embody in order to be living your dream? Who do you need to become? Make a list or identify that one quality. Look deeper again, what is in the way of you embodying these things? It could be things like: unworthiness, unlovable, not enough-ness. What do you carry around like a badge that is simply not true, but you were taught otherwise? Take a dive into the deeper stories that you tell yourself. Let them rip - list them out on a piece of paper, write them all as they occur to you. List here things like anger or guilt. Find any reason still in your unconscious that you don't step into your dreams.

Do not try to figure them out, or analyze them or even defend them. Simply list them. Keep going. Set a timer for 5 minutes and write away. Then when you feel complete with the list, find 5 more. Yes, they are there. What can you now release in order to step into who you are? These are very important and we usually have some resistance to them. Oh, and be sure to write down resistance.

When your list feels complete, ask yourself, if you are willing to release these things. Are you willing to let them go, right here and right now in order to live the life that you dream of? If so, tear the sheet up into little shreds and say, "These things no longer have any power over me. I am free. I am love. I am enough. I am deserving. I am worthy." Shake it off. Move your body and feel the spaciousness that was created in this exercise.

Remembering that nature abhors a vacuum, now fill the space with the Truth! Use the affirmations I gave you above and create your own. What is the truth about you? Use the I AM. Write for another 5 minutes and fill another page.

Now, come back to your vision. Begin to write it in present tense as you'd love to see it. Use feeling words and invoke your senses. "I'm so happy and grateful now that I can taste the fulfillment of running my marathon." How does that feel? Exciting? Expansive? We call this the first force. Laying, claiming and defining your dreams.

Sometimes what happens is that our baseline level of existence jumps in and says, "Whoa, wait, you can't do that or have that!" and we end up giving up on our goals and dreams. Let's STOP doing that! Gay Hendricks speaks to this phenomenon in his book, *The Big Leap*. If you haven't read it yet, check it out.

Disappointment, Frustration and Irritation

After we've had a breakthrough experience whether in consciousness or life itself, it is natural to feel let down after then initial euphoria. It's the drop after the adrenaline rush. It is our subconscious calling us back to what we've known. It's the classic upper level limit that Gay Hendricks talks about. It can show up as a feeling of being disappointed. Maybe my dream isn't really mine. Maybe things didn't go as planned and I'm disappointed. Irritation is a classic favorite of mine. I find myself slightly irritated by something or someone. It's like a rash, a slight irritation that if not treated immediately can turn into frustration and worse.

Frustration, irritation and disappointment lead to a downward spiral of emotion. It is a bit like a virus. If left to its own devices, it can grow and fester. Frustration blocks the flow of energy in and through your body. Irritation prevents seeing the blessings. Disappointment leaves an aftertaste that prevents us from fully enjoying life. Realize that it could simply be the reaction to stepping out into your dreams. Become more interested in the dream, the desire. Let the emotions go and choose again.

16

Accessing the Subconscious

The subconscious is that which builds the foundation of our lives, the fabric of our being. It is where everything we have ever experienced, heard, seen or been told is stored. The subconscious is like a huge mega computer. It does not know the difference in time or truth. It stores beliefs, emotions, reactions and with repetition creates our life patterns.

For example, when you were young you might have had an experience, it could have been yours or you could have witnessed it in your family. Perhaps you were neglected one time as a baby, when your care givers were busy with something else. The event was stored in your subconscious, along with the meaning you gave it. This is very important. What we make things mean is subjective and can be different for every person, even in the same situation.

We call this meaning making. Events are neutral, but it is our interpretation and our history that tells us they mean something. We decide if things are good or bad, if they support our *beingness* or they diminish our well-being and worth. The process takes place over time and creates patterns and beliefs, that then inform us of who we are and what's ok and what is not ok. Much of our self-worth comes from simple neutral events happening while we are very, very young and our subconscious strings them together to make them mean something about us.

Eventually, something else happens and you felt neglect again. The subconscious will link them together. Now, you are beginning to build a pattern as this happens over and over. The pattern is reinforced, becomes a trigger, and over time a contract or vow might be made. Maybe the baby heard the words in a moment of exhaustion from a parent "Oh you are so much work!" We can imagine that a parent could say that, without meaning anything except raising a baby is hard work. But that baby takes it on. Then she hears similar but different statements over time. It could be things like "why did you do that?" "oh I can't deal with this right now." "Just stop" or "you're too much." Why did I spill the milk? Only because it was an accident. The question is only a question, but the subconscious links the emotion experienced together to create a belief statement like "I'm too much work, I make life hard for my parents."

Can you see where we are going? Perhaps one day something happens and that baby, who is now a toddler says to him/herself, "Obviously I'm too much work, so I will never.... Or I will always... I will never rely on anyone else. I will always take care of everything from this moment forward." And that is now the pattern and trigger. Remember this is all in the subconscious mind, we are not aware that is happening.

So fast forward 30 or 40 or 50 years and this same adult has the belief that "I'm not worthy," or "I have to do it all myself" or "No one cares" or "Life is a struggle."

When we begin to do our clearing work, we learn how to identify the patterns and triggers. When the trigger gets triggered, the pattern kicks into place. This is how and why so many of us who are healthy adults revert back to old behaviors, especially when around extended family situations. When we get triggered, everything in us says, remember the contract you made when you were just a wee baby. Be careful... Protect... Never... Always....

As we identify the patterns, we can explore them. They are apparent in our lives, but we aren't typically conscious of why they are there or what to do about them. They show up in repeated places. You see them and think to yourself, why is everybody the same? I get the same results in each relationship, in each job, in each event. This is the subconscious playing out its role impeccably.

Now to change it. First, identify the pattern, follow it around and see all the layers of it. Dig deep, track it back. Look with curiosity, rather than judgment, at what the triggers are; at what happens and what the deep seated unconscious belief is that is being played out.

Track that belief back to its inception, to the central core of the origination and bring it out into the light. Once we see and identify a pattern, it is easier to shift. Trail it all the way back to its beginning and pull that event, that moment, the contract or vow that was made, into the light of conscious awareness. When we get to the core and begin to play with it, the entire structure of belief and patterns can dismantle very easily and quickly.

Think of a spider web. If you catch an outer layer of the web, it sticks and is hard to get off. You can get to it layer by layer, but if you can get right in there and grab the center it will collapse. This is what we are doing in the subconscious.

Have a dialog with the emotion, the originating event and the pattern. Acknowledge that it has protected you for all these years. Thank it for doing its job and renegotiate with it. If you can bring it all the way into the light and renegotiate it, it is transcended. You will then need to create and plant the new belief. Find one that works for you, that resonates with a deeper part of your soul.

"Life is a struggle," could become: "Life supports me. Life is easy. Life is fun. Life is an adventure." Take it like new medicine. Taste it, feel it, hear it, become it. Ingest the new belief into your being by repeating it, by becoming it, by resonating to the vibrational frequency that it emanates. Ahhh. Look up to the sky and allow it to be poured into you, filling all the interspaces of your being with a new nectar.

Working with the subconscious is delicious, it is magical, insightful and transformational. There is a lot of clearing work you can do on your own. However, the deeper patterns and core beliefs are much easier to clear with a facilitator. That's because it is unconscious and the conscious mind cannot do it. We actually have to access the subconscious in order to make lasting changes.

Clearing the subconscious is a spiritual practice. It can be grueling and painful or it can be easy, quick and gentle. It is the most profound journey of all time and that which leads to true awakening.

Our emotions are energy in motion and they also indicate the state that we are in. Dr. David R. Hawkins, MD, PhD developed a "map" of the levels of human consciousness (also called the Scale of Consciousness). His basic premise is that emotional state indicates where we are in spiritual unfoldment. His scale is well documented and is included in his book, *Power VS Force*.

Shame, guilt, apathy, grief, fear, desire, anger, pride, courage, neutrality, willingness, acceptance, reason, love, joy, peace and enlightenment. Each state or stage is a layer of growth that we move through. That does not mean that we don't touch emotions in every stage on any given day, but his science is that this is a progressive spectrum of spiritual growth and unfoldment.

Abraham Hicks also refers to an emotional scale; however, this is one that is progressed through on an emotional basis only. Meaning that moving up the scale of emotions is possible on any given day. It does not refer to states of consciousness or spiritual unfoldment, only the emotion presently being felt.

EMOTIONAL SCALE:

1. Joy / Knowledge / Empowerment / Freedom / Love / Appreciation
2. Passion
3. Enthusiasm / Eagerness / Happiness
4. Positive Expectation / Belief
5. Optimism
6. Hopefulness
7. Contentment
8. Boredom
9. Pessimism
10. Frustration / Irritation / Impatience
11. Overwhelmed
12. Disappointment
13. Doubt
14. Worry
15. Blame
16. Discouragement
17. Anger
18. Revenge
19. Hatred / Rage
20. Jealousy
21. Insecurity / Guilt / Unworthiness
22. Fear / Grief / Depression / Despair / Powerlessness

[As found in Esther and Jerry Hicks' book, *Ask and It is Given*, page 114.]

This scale gives us a road map for moving up. The basis for both David Hawkins and Abraham Hicks is that the further up the scale you are, the better you feel. Quite simple actually.

When you find yourself down lower on the scale, please, please remember, there is nothing wrong and you are not broken. It only means you are in an emotional state. It is normal and natural. It matters not where we find ourselves on the emotional scale. There is no judgment. When life happens, we find ourselves wherever we are. We've all been depressed, angry, frustrated, perhaps hopeless at times. The goal when you are lower on the scale is simply to move up one or two notches. To find relief from where you are and to move to better.

Take a breath and acknowledge where you are, allow the feelings you are experiencing to have free rein for a bit. Stop, take a look, feel them, name them and allow them. From allowing them, come to the place of accepting them. "Oh, look at this. I'm feeling hopeless right now." Become curious. "Oh, that's curious. Wonder what that's about?" Look gently with curiosity. "Hmmm. Ok. What does hopeless feel like? Where in my body does it live?" Does it have a color or shape? Can you draw it out in front of you into a container? What does that container look like? Can you allow it? Can you accept it? Can you pick it up? Can you lift it to eye level? Up higher? Can you release it up into the universe? If so, what do you find underneath it? Is it another emotion? If so, look at it, feel it, name it and allow it. Repeat the process of identifying and containing the next layer of emotion and see if you can lift it. Keep exploring the layers, if you have the time and space to do so, until you find a spaciousness.

When you find relief or spaciousness, bask.

Feel the freedom and peace that arises in spaciousness.

If you haven't found space yet, no worries. Simply feel the emotion, name it, allow it with curiosity then allow it to lift just a bit. What do you find underneath it? It could be a step up on the emotional scale, or it could be something else entirely.

When our emotions are not allowed and felt through to completion, they get packed down into our subconscious in a similar way that the layers of rock create our mountains and land. If you've ever studied geology or been out in nature where you can see the different layers, you'll have a sense of what I'm talking about.

In emotional clearing, we become geologists. We become curious as we excavate. Why would we excavate? To release the layers of rock, the heavy, constricting prison of layers of rock that keep us stuck and feeling heavy. As we excavate the deep and heavy emotional patterns and states of being from our unconscious, we are freed up to experience peace, love, joy and fulfillment. We are freed up to let the light that we are out to shine for the entire world to see! We are freed to Be.

The emotional body is designed to be a fluid body, one that functions optimally when it is allowed to flow. Remember emotions are energy in motion; E-Motion. They are meant to flow, but when they become sediment-ed, solid like a layer of rock in the earth, they cause us pain and suffering. When you find yourself stuck in an emotion that doesn't want to move (the lower ones can become quite dense and heavy), see if you can move up one simple step.

When you find yourself on the lower end of the scale it will be nearly impossible to make a jump from the bottom to the top of the scale. That's why is it called scale. For example, if you find yourself in jealousy (#20 in this chart), feel into the jealousy until you can lift it just a bit. See if you can find rage and notice if there is a bit of relief in the rage. From rage, can you find revenge? Then anger? Do you see how moving up one step at a time can be helpful and bring relief from the current state? This is stepping.

Then there is the quantum leap that we've been referring to. While it is true that it is hard to step from discouragement to appreciation in little steps, it is also quite possible to activate the frequency of gratitude and appreciation, even from the lower states.

Let's play both stepping and the quantum leap with the emotion of discouragement. *Activate it by remembering a time when you were discouraged. Look for it, feel it in your body and allow it. Accept that it is there. Here's a little trick. We cannot make it go away, it is not about denying it or pushing it out of our systems. The magic comes in allowing it, accepting it and then transcending it. Do not try to make emotions leave. They won't leave, they will only get stuck. Let discouragement come alive in you. You recognize it, it has a familiar feeling to it. Now step it up. As you allow discouragement, choose instead blame.* NOTE: Why would you want to be in blame? Isn't that icky? Remember, no judgements on any emotions, they are simply energy trapped. Blame in and of itself does not feel good, but coming from discouragement, because it is a step up, it feels better. Better is what we are going for. *Then step up to worry.* This is the stepping process. Often it takes time.

Let's go back to discouragement. Activate it again, allow it to be in your awareness. How does it feel? What does it look like? Because we can, let's activate the frequency of gratitude. Think of something that you are grateful for. It could be the sun, or breeze, or the fact that you are breathing. Simply activate gratitude. Find it, remember a time when you were truly grateful. Feel the activation in your body. What is happening? Stay with it for a few minutes. If you drop out of gratitude, activate it again. Use the energy and image of activation. Turning it on. Calling it in. Come into a vibration of gratitude and notice what you notice. Do you feel lighter? Are you in resistance to it? If so, take another few breaths. Perhaps you notice your breathing change? Perhaps your shoulders drop or tension is released. Let gratitude wash over your entire being. Bask in it. This is the quantum leap.

17

In the Midst of Life

We have all had life circumstances that have brought us to the edge, where we didn't know where to turn, how to breathe or even if we could get up in the morning. For me, one of those times was when my son was 14 and he was in the throes of a court mandated in-patient drug treatment program five hours from my home. I was so deeply involved in the details and minutia of my life and his that I couldn't sleep, I couldn't eat, I could hardly breathe. I was scared, wracked with fear. I was guilty - what I had done to create this in his life? I was filled with shame and blame and guilt and I was terrified at what this event might mean for me and for my son.

I have such compassion for anyone dealing with drugs or addiction. It is a tough path and one that will wring you out the way you wring out a sponge after using it. It will push and pull you to the ends of what you think you can handle and then give you some more to handle. You will feel emotions that you didn't even know existed and you don't even have words for. You will be turned inside out and scrubbed with a stainless steel Brillo pad. It's not fun, it's not easy and it totally sucks. So if you are there, or anywhere else that is squeezing you beyond what you think you can take, you have my empathy and my compassion. But what I know to be true is this: you will get through it. You will be able to take another breath and get up in the morning one more day. You will be able to take the next step and then the next. Put yourself first, take care of you, get the support you need through friends, professionals and groups.

This goes for anyone who is dealing with intense situations. I'm thinking of some people close to me right now dealing with the grit of tough life. It happens. It is life on this planet. It will stretch you, pull you, push you to the edges and then push some more.

Please, please, please, get support. Join a support group of others dealing with similar things. I joined a Tough Love group during my son's adventures in drugs and juvenile court. I'm certain it saved my life and quite possibly his. (By the way, he is a fully functioning, responsible, loving and caring adult now.) It gave me both direction and strength to do what I needed to do. Feel your feelings. Let them rip, appropriately. Feeling your feelings fully allows them to burn like fuel on a fire. Stuffing them, denying them or otherwise not allowing the emotions to move imbeds them in your body and consciousness. Don't do that.

If you need support in feeling, get that! Go sit in your car and feel them - let the tears flow, let the anger burn. Yell and scream if you have to - into a pillow if you need to muffle the sound. Do some intense physical activity. During another period in my life when I was being stretched and pulled during a divorce, I was so angry that I couldn't see straight. I did not want my young children to witness it, so I swam. I swam laps at a local pool and screamed underwater over and over again. I played racquetball and imagined a certain person's face on that little blue ball that I was smacking again and again. Eventually my anger ran its course and then I was free to take authentic action.

When we bury our emotions, they actually run us. They have control because we use so much energy in keeping them under control that they win. Again, if you are in an intense situation, get the support that you need.

We are not meant to live life alone. We are here to be in community and connection. Especially if you are a woman, you are wired to be supported, to be witnessed and to witness. Over the decades of facilitating groups, classes, retreats and other gatherings, I have found consistently and across the board it is the connection with others that creates the pathways for healing, the strength to go on and the courage to do what needs to be done.

When we are in a group, whether it is a support group, a workshop or a retreat situation, most people come in feeling alone and unique, separate and different. When there is a safe place and space created for true and authentic sharing, magic happens. People realize that they are not the only ones feeling what they are feeling or going through what they are going through. People take great comfort in authentic sharing.

I was in a group recently where something happened that opened the veils of authentic connection. The woman who initiated it immediately said, "Oh I shouldn't have said that… it was cheesy or slimy or some such thing." The other woman who was in the conversation said, “Oh no, that was the most authentic thing yet – it touched my heart and opened me to you.” What happened is that they got real. Both of them. The first woman got real and then immediately pulled back, thinking that was too much or “Why did I say that?” The second woman felt the “real” and responded. It touched her heart and allowed her to also go real. There is magic in that. In this particular situation there was some training involved so we got to talk about the experience. It was amazing and we all learned so much.

People want to be real and authentic, but we often hold back. People want to see real and authentic and when they do, the space opens up for more authentic connection. How do you find peace? Be You. Be real. Be present.

18

The End

It's going to be alright. I promise you. What I can also promise is that you will have challenges along the way and that you will eventually leave this body for the next expression of life. You will die and so will your loved ones. But what if that isn't wrong or bad? Of course, most of us will have heartbreak and our foundations will be rocked when a loved one dies. We will get to walk through grief, for however long that takes. We will then learn a new way of being, hopefully with our hearts broken wide open and life will go on.

What if we remove the "wrongness" from death? Who wants to live on the planet forever, anyway? Now, my preference is that my friends and family stick around for a long, long, long time. That nothing bad happens to them. That they live lives full of ease and success and happiness.

A friend of ours died yesterday. This man fought a long, hard fight with the challenges his body was having. He was diagnosed with cancer about 4 years ago and underwent treatment. He then had a surgery for back issues and was left paralyzed. The doctors told him, he'd never walk again. Then he walked again. Then they found another cancer. Last week, after he'd been in the hospital for a few weeks, the doctors said he was well enough to go home. Wednesday, he went home. Friends were out visiting with him on the patio Thursday evening. He was full of life and planning for the future. He died that night at 10 pm. At his home, with his wife, after having just been released from the hospital because he was doing so well.

Was that wrong? Was that failure? I don't think so. Is it hard for his wife? Of course! For his friends? Yes, of course. Did he do it wrong? No! Was he broken? No - even as his body was deteriorating. He and his soul were good!

Remember our quote? "Everything is going to be alright in the end. If it's not yet alright, do not worry, it is not yet the end."

I believe at the end of life as we know it, is the beginning of something quite eternal, that has been going on for long before our soul was born into this life and this body. I believe that our time here on the planet is a smidgen of our existence, that we have experiences here then move on. That does not eliminate our human suffering in the death of a loved one, especially in tough circumstances and tragedy, but it does say grief is an emotion that will pass with time. I also believe that any heart break we experience in life can lead us to a wider, more open heart, giving us more capacity to love and therefore, live even more fully.

No one regrets, at the end of their lives that they didn't spend more time at work. What people regret is not what they did, but what they didn't do - the adventures they could have taken, the deeper, more intimate conversations they could have had. Loving more. Spending time with family and friends. Enjoying life, stopping to smell the roses, laying in the sun, reveling in nature. Some regret dreams that are still dormant, unfulfilled deep within their hearts and souls. Make the commitment to yourself to live with no regrets! Do what makes your heart sing; love fully, live out loud, enjoy life to its fullest. Do it today, not later, for tomorrow is not promised.

The Dragon

There is a story about a man going to a psychiatrist because there was a huge dragon living under his bed and he was scared. He was terrified and didn't know what to do about it. So he went to this doctor and told him the story. The doctor said, "I think I can cure you of this terror, but you will have to come to me three times a week for three months to begin to get results." The doctor never heard from him again, until years later when they ran into each other. Because of the uniqueness of the case, the doctor remembered and asked the man what had happened to him? He replied, "I was more terrified of the money it would cost me to come to you than the dragon, so I went home and made friends with him."

Make friends with your dragons.

What is your dragon? Where do you live with fear still present? Over the past couple of years, I've been leaving my profession as a church minister. I had been doing that for a long time, over 16 years and also had lived with the impulse to go outside the church walls. When I finally made the break, and started off on my own, so to speak, I encountered yet another layer of fear.

Within the context of minister, I was good at what I did, I am a fabulous teacher and facilitator and speaker. I have deep compassion for people and the tools to guide them. So, I thought it would be an easy leap into a new arena. What I discovered is the amount of identity I had wrapped up in my title and the safety of the sanctuary container. I had a set audience, the congregation, and I served them well. Now, those container walls are gone and I'm standing much more vulnerable, authentic and raw than ever before.

I'm having the feeling that I'm now doing what I was teaching all along. Everything in my life has led me to this point. My fear was triggered by leaving the container, leaving the mantle of minister and stepping outside of the relative safety and support of the church movement I was in. I was called to leave the next of familiarity and comfort. Where are you called? What is stopping you now?

There is resistance in our collective consciousness to stepping out into the unknown. It doesn't mean anything, except that it's there. The question is what are you going to do with the fear that shows up for you? Are you going to let it continue to run the show? Or are you going to turn around, face it, feel it and move on without it? It is a choice and it is a process, but once you have done it, it becomes easier both to spot and to shift.

Imagine now for a moment, life with no fear. Imagine the complete and total freedom to be and do exactly what you are called to be and do in any moment. Imagine there is nothing stopping you. Slide into freedom to be. Notice what you notice. How does that feel?

Imagine truly living the life you are here to live, filled with your genius, love, grace and so much fun! Imagine that you are doing exactly what you love to do with people you love and appreciate. Imagine that life on the planet is a grand adventure. Your life has not gotten easier, but more rich and fulfilling too. What does it look like and feel like? What's stopping you now?

19

The If-Only Drain is a psychological vampire that loves to suck the life force right out of your dreams by keeping you stuck in a victim mode to your own life. Perhaps you've made its acquaintance at some point along your life. It can show up like:

If only....

- I was older
- I was younger
- I was married
- I was single
- I had kids
- The kids were grown and on their own
- I'd gone to school when I'd had the chance
- I hadn't married/divorced/ him
- I'd made a different choice a decade (or 5) ago
- I was prettier
- I was thinner
- I was healthier
- I was richer
- I mattered
- They understood me better
- They...he...she...did or did not do what they did
- I had better support

Perhaps you can add your own, because you recognize the flavor of "If-Only". If only is not only a vampire, but also a prison. It's time to let it go! The thing is that when we let go of the prisons that keeps us small and we release the victim within, life changes. And when life changes, everything changes.

Are you up for it? Are you sure? At what point does the risk of playing full out exceed the cost of playing small? Spend some time with this question, because it can change everything and will impact everyone close to you.

"Life should not be a journey to the grave with the intention of arriving safely in a pretty and well preserved body, but rather to skid in broadside in a cloud of smoke, thoroughly used up, totally worn out, and loudly proclaiming "Wow! What a Ride!"
-Hunter S. Thompson

What if you lived life full out, what if you lived with no regrets? What if you knew you could not fail? What would you do then? My friend and colleague, Mindy Audlin wrote a book, *"What If It All Goes Right?"*, you might enjoy along this idea. What if your idea worked? What if you succeeded? What if it is all working out?

What if it all goes right and you find ease? Removing the "if-Only" drain is one simple way to discover a life of greater ease, more freedom in your thought and a greater expression of who you are here to be.

Untying the Knots of Nots

Are you all tied up in knots? Or are you all tied up in "nots"? The "have nots," the "can nots," the "will nots?"

Are you stressed and overwhelmed? Tired and exhausted? What would you need to release and be freed up from? Do you even believe that you could be? Take a deep breath and imagine what it might feel like to be freed. What would you have to give up? What would you have to release? What is the payoff for being tied up in knots? Remember the yarn analogy in the **Creating Space** chapter?

For me, I've been untying knots (and nots) for decades. Each time I untie a knot that has kept me small and safe, I've stepped into a whole new way of being. I've had my own quantum leap, conscious evolution jumps. Each and every one of them had risk to it, required strength or courage and took me places I hadn't even dreamed of. Each untying left me exposed and vulnerable, and with more access to the light and love that was in me. Some of our leaps come by nature; when we are a child, then a grown up; when we have babies then become empty nesters. When we go to work and retire. Moving across the country, or changing jobs. All of these times are opportunities to do something different. Take a chance, let loose and fly!

Before I went to seminary, I had already taken some great quantum risks. I had already had careers as a computer programmer, a massage therapist and was working as an office administrator when the call came in so strongly I had to listen. I had moved across country a few times and I was at the time a single mom with two kids ages 9 & 13. Some say it was courageous and brave to take these risks. For me, it was more like I was ignorant or innocent. Little did I know or care, even, how tough it might be. I was committed to following my inner north star, the impulse within that said go. I trust it. I listen to it, (usually.) When I was called into ministry, it was a huge and life changing step. Prior to answering that call, I was shy and quiet. I did not like to speak in front of people and although I knew I had deep thoughts about life and things, I wasn't prone to share them.

The call I received over 10 years later to leave ministry (the first time) was an even greater risk. It was profound in the surrender and trust that it took to do that portion of my life, a deep spiritual pilgrimage of letting everything go. Then last year, after returning to serve in a church again for a few years, I left the ministry again. I'm answering a call to serve creation in a deeper, broader way. It seemed like a good idea, that it would be an easy transition from church to entrepreneur and it continues to be a journey of moving from struggle to ease, from contained and contracted to expansive.

We are always either contracting or expanding.

The writing of this book is a vital step in the journey.

With each step, knots of being are untied and new expansive ways are evolved. Each takes a risk, a stepping off the edge of what is known to something unknown. We all have it, the call to more... more purpose, more passion, more connection. Will you risk it? Will you take that step off the ledge and fly?

What are your knots of nots today? Take a look and begin to unravel them. Take action today to begin to free yourself from your bondage to find liberation and freedom, to express the greater, more expanded version of you. Loose the knot of the anchor that keeps you moored, the one that keeps you safe in the harbor of your life, even as you yearn to sail the open seas.

We are here to make manifest the glory of Self, to experience Love and wholeness. We are here to continue evolving to a deeper and more meaningful existence. We are here to move from the mass consciousness of separation to the universal consciousness of Oneness. Are you ready?

20

From Separation to Oneness

Separation is a state of being, albeit illusionary. It is the experience and foundation for our life on planet earth. As we evolved along the spiral of creation from the beginning of time, at each stage change there was a quantum leap. In the beginning when there was nothing at all, came an impulse that was so great it caused a leap into light. From darkness to light. And creation began. There were quantum leaps into greater life - single cell organisms that had life; to multiple-cell organisms that led to plant and animal life. From that there was an impulse so great that humanity was created.

There is currently an impulse so great for the next level of experience and expression that we are on the verge of collectively leaping from the separated human to the Universal Human. Barbara Marx Hubbard and the Conscious Evolution movement guide us through an exploration of the evolutionary leap from the separated human experience to the Universal Human, the experience of knowing oneness. This comes from the scientific world, as well as the spiritual and ancient cultures. Science, spirituality and ancient traditions converge at this point and it is brilliant! You can read more in Barbara's book, *Conscious Evolution*.

As the Universal Human we will discover, not as an intellectual awareness, but as an experience from the depths of our being, a sense of wholeness, of belonging, of peace. In this new consciousness there will be no room for separation, judgment, lack or limitation of any kind.

We are the forerunners, the way-showers. As we come into a dimensional shift, we land in a new place. This is the beginning and we are well into the beginning. The more that we land here, the more that we come to live and move and have our beings here, the more the collective will catch up.

The Universal Human will look the same on the outside, but will experience life quite differently. We will shift from separation to wholeness, from aloneness to collective connection. All sense of lack and limitation will be replaced with abundance and expansion. Poverty will be a thing of the past, because as we come into new ways of seeing and being it will be eradicated. War and violence will no longer be a constant on our planet. If we know we are One with all people, we would not kill or fight. We would not be afraid of each other and our differences, there would be safety in Oneness.

Politics will change, governments will change, foreign policy will change. We will become truly a global community. The children that are being born right now, have seeds of this new consciousness. I was talking with my friend last Christmas about her five-year-old grandson. They were watching the global route of Santa delivering gifts around the world. Every time they named a country, he responded with something like, "That's my world." His universal consciousness and global perspective was profound at such a young age. He didn't see separate countries or states; it is all one big world to him. Santa is in London - that's my world. Santa is in Germany - that's my world. Santa is in Greenland - that's my world.

I love that so much, because it indicates a new consciousness that is coming - we are not separated by state or country lines, or continents even. We are One! We are One with all that is! We are connected by the very life force that sustains us.

Do you know that beautiful Aspen groves are all one tree? It appears to be many hundreds of individual trees, but it is all one root system. It's a mind blowing concept to realize that we are like that too. We are not alone. Yes, we are individualized expressions of the One Creation. Yes, we live and express individually, but it is all one humanity.

Remember when, not all that long ago, our country's founding fathers did not believe that blacks or women were as valuable as white men? Remember not that long ago, many people on this planet were fighting for their rights to life, liberty and the pursuit of happiness. And right now, in other countries in the world, women are still considered a lesser species, are still fighting for their rights to an education.

Malala Yousafzai, a teenage Pakistani activist for female education and the youngest-ever Nobel Prize laureate, fought for her rights to education. A few years ago, she was shot in the face in an assassination attempt. Her story flew across the world in an up-rage against education discrimination, but it is not her story alone. It is rampant still. You can read about her story in her book, *I Am Malala: The Girl Who Stood Up for Education and Was Shot by the Taliban*.

Most of you reading this book are probably women. Thank you to the men who are joining us! We still fight for equal rights and equal pay. I saw a video recently of young children from ages 4-8, who were asked to do chores. Washing windows, putting away dishes, etc., at the end, the girls were given less money that the boys. Across the board, both the boys and the girls were like – that's not right, that's not fair.

In our country people who love people of the same sex are still being highly discriminated against. Even as we legalize same-sex marriage, others are being blatantly refused and bullied. I have two friends and colleagues, who just this week, were brutally and verbally abused and kicked out of a local restaurant, simply because they appeared to be gay. It blows my mind that some people are still so fearful and discriminatory.

As we come into our Wholeness as a collective, as we make the cosmic quantum leap experiencing separation to knowing Oneness, those differences will drop away. We will find not only equality and recognize our sameness, but we will also celebrate our uniqueness and individuality without threat or judgment.

It is happening right now. We are One, we are whole, we are complete. Now to realize it fully. To come into complete experience of this, we have to let go of, surrender, release all that is unlike love and Oneness. Every time we release an experience of separation, we come to realize wholeness more completely. Every time we come to experience wholeness more completely, something else drops away and we come into a greater ease in our body, minds and life. Can you feel what happens when you release the tension of being and holding yourself separate, and relax into Oneness? There is a softening of all systems, a quickening of life force and a deep soul relaxation that is automatic.

Coming to know Oneness is a simple shift that will change everything. To know that you are love and love alone. To come into an experience of the Oneness. We can touch it any time, it is already there. Touch it again and again. Each time it anchors more deeply into your awareness. Right now. Come with me. Join me in one simple shift that can change everything.

Experiencing Oneness. *Close your eyes and do some deep breathing. Feel your body sinking into the chair that you are sitting in. Become aware of the breath that you are breathing. Feel it entering and exiting your body with each inhale and exhale. Are you breathing or are you being breathed? Become aware of the air permeating and penetrating your entire being, both inside and outside. You are enveloped in the air, just like everyone else. Imagine a person across the globe breathing the same air that you are. Feel your feet connecting to the ground below you. Draw your awareness down through your feet and into the ground, breathing up all that the earth has to support you. Feel your roots sinking deep into the planet, just like everyone else. Take a look at your body, each organ, muscle, bone. As separate and individual as they are, they compose You, your body, one organism. As we are each individual and unique on the planet, all together, we comprise humanity, one species. We are not separate from each other or the planet. We are one, all together.*

Feel the expansive nature of this thought. We are one with the cosmos and the universe. We are connected by the breath we breathe, just as our bodies are connected by connected tissue. Become One with all that is. Become One with the earth and the sun. Feel the connection with a person across the globe. One heart, One humanity. Bask in this awareness of connection. We are One.

21

Get Your Gratitude On

It is easy to be grateful when things are going well, but how do you do when life is happening and the challenges are pushing and pulling you all over the place?

Why gratitude? Why are we talking about gratitude in the midst of suffering and ease and evolution? Gratitude is the glue that ties it all together. Gratitude is the nourishing and nurturing vibration that activates the growth. Like *Miracle-Gro* for your plants.

Gratitude is for your life,
like Miracle-Gro is for your plants.

Gratitude is an energy and frequency that both allows for more and calls in more! It is an activating frequency, not passive. On the emotional scale Gratitude, Appreciation and Love are the top three vibrations. They put us as close to God or Creation as we can get, while still in human form.

Scientifically and pragmatically, gratitude is the vibrational energy that brings your mind and heart in closer touch with Spirit, it draws the mind from what is wrong to what is right. Gratitude changes your body chemistry, your mind and keeps your heart free from worry and distraction.

Practice getting your gratitude on as often as you can remember it. Set a timer on your watch or cell phone for every hour. Each time the timer goes off, activate gratitude consciously, from wherever you are. Not to ignore or make wrong, but simply to activate that which you desire more.

If you have food in your fridge, clothes on your back, a roof over your head and a place to sleep you are richer than 75% of the world.
If you have money in the bank, your wallet, and some spare change you are among the top 8% of the world's wealthy.
If you woke up this morning with more health than illness you are more blessed than the million people who will not survive this week.
If you have never experienced the danger of battle, the agony of imprisonment or torture, or the horrible pangs of starvation you are luckier than 500 million people alive and suffering.
If you hold up your head with a smile on your face and are truly thankful, you are blessed because the majority can, but most do not.
If you can read this message you are more fortunate than 3 billion people in the world who cannot read it at all.
- Author Unknown

Can you feel the gratitude rising up in you reading these statistics? We have so much to be grateful for and when we practice gratitude it increases. Yes, most of us have lots that we feel ungrateful for also, but shift your focus, find the gratitude as an exercise, as a spiritual practice and as a way of being. You'll be so glad when you do!

Let's activate gratitude now. No matter what is going on in your life, no matter what your reactions are to the reading of this book, close your eyes and become grateful. Find a comfortable place to sit and set a timer for 10 minutes. Yes, you can afford 10 minutes out of your busy day - it just might change everything. *Close your eyes and take a deep breath in. Feel the air entering your body. Feel gratitude for oxygen and the ability to breathe. Become aware of your body. How does it feel? Are there places of tension or tightness? Be grateful that you have a body, for the alternative is to not be alive at all. Become aware of the room you are sitting in. Be grateful for the roof over your head and the chair you are sitting on. Think about what you had to eat already today or a meal that is coming up. Be grateful that you have enough food to eat - much of the world does not. Think about your bed and how yummy it is to sink into the sheets beneath the covers at the end of the day. How grateful are you for the bed?*

Put a smile on your face and feel the gratitude bubbling up from the center of your being, overflowing to the tips of your toes and fingers. Feel it rising up to the top of your head. Notice what is happening in your body. Do you feel differently? Still with your eyes closed, bring gratitude to your life situations. Even to the challenging ones and see what happens. I'm so grateful. I'm so blessed. Say these two statements to yourself a few times. Let them activate another level of gratitude. Say them out loud and claim them as true. I'm so grateful. I'm so blessed. And so it is.

22

Why We Are On the Planet

Why are we here? What is this life all about anyway? Without going all philosophical or religious on you, we are here to make manifest the glory of God.

You are a child of God. Your playing small does not serve the world. There's nothing enlightened about shrinking so that other people won't feel insecure around you. We were born to make manifest the glory of God that is within us. It's not just in some of us; it's in everyone. And as we let our own light shine, we unconsciously give other people permission to do the same. As we are liberated from our own fear, Our presence automatically liberates others.
—Marianne Williamson

We were born to make manifest the glory of God that is within us. As we let our own light shine, we give other people permission to do the same. We are here to experience life and to express the light and love that is within us. God is light and God is Love, when we express love and light, we make manifest the glory of God. Life includes polarities: light and dark, good and bad, warm and cold. So we choose at some level to come experience life. How can you experience the sweetness of forgiveness without the bitterness of betrayal? How can you experience the relief of a long awaited homecoming without having been lost or alone? How can you know peace in your soul without having experienced the lack of or opposite of peace?

How can you recognize the brightness of your light without having experienced darkness? You can't. It would only be theory. We are here to experience and integrate all of our experiences. There is not good or bad, there is only experience. When we discover that experience is what we are having and recognize that which is within us as wanting to be expressed, the rules change. We become much more interested in being and bringing our fullest selves to the world. We become much more interested in how we can contribute our individual gifts, talents and passions in a way that serves the greater good. We become more interested in that which lifts and expands us than in the other stuff of life.

As we awaken to the Truth of our Being, we discover the deeper impulse of creation itself moving in and through us. It is calling us, pushing us and pulling us to a greater expression. The deeper impulse is called Vocational Arousal, the awakening of your Soul purpose and the activation of the desire to create. It is the recognizing of the unique combination of gifts, passions and expressions of that which you are becoming. It has taken each and every one of your life experiences to bring you to this moment. Now, what are you going to do with them? Are you ready to activate a new possibility and expression?

We live on the planet at a very opportune time. For the existence of humanity, we have lived in the world of separation. Humanity had to separate from the whole in order to experience itself. Then we forgot that separation was the illusion, was the play that we were acting in and we began to believe in it.

Right now, we have the opportunity to wake up from the dream of illusion of separation and remember Oneness. We do that through Love. We do that by awakening again and again to our Wholeness, releasing and transcending all else. We do it by consciously choosing to believe in love and wholeness even with the evidence of fear, lack and separation.

When we do that, we come out. We recognize the unique and individualized expressions as colors of the rainbow that we are part of. We celebrate our uniqueness and others as well. We find ways to play together to create anew. We blend from our wholeness with others who are whole, creating new colors and possibilities for ourselves and the planet.

In our wholeness, our old beliefs and patterns no longer serve us. In the chapter, **Believe it Because We See it? Or See it Because We Believe it?**, we looked at beliefs that were ready to be surrendered. Let's take another look at some new beliefs that we can install now.

Try on these new beliefs:

- Life is meant to be good
- Life is a grand adventure
- I'm on a hero's journey to find myself
- God is good, all the time
- Creation is ever expanding and so am I

- I love my life and life loves me
- I choose love
- I choose peace
- I feel my feelings all the way through to completion
- My feelings are only energy in motion, they do not define who I am

Let's look again – why do I believe this? Be the investigator of your life. Can you apply the same investigative questioning to new beliefs? What happens now?

The universe is supporting an awakening. Awaken to love. Awaken to your Self. It doesn't mean that you won't have life situations and circumstances that knock the wind out of you, but it does mean that you will know you are not alone, that you are supported, that you are One and that this too will pass.

It will mean that you have new tools, beliefs, patterns of being that bring a lightness to the world. It will mean you have the feeling of flow, that you have given up struggle and suffering (or at least most of it) and that you know Love and Peace and Joy. It will mean that you find fulfillment, freedom and contentment.

And then you are free. You are One. You can discover the glory of your Soul and the glory of conscious co-creation.

The end of separation comes when we realize that it is an illusion; and when you know that in the cells of your being, everything changes. It's just in our hiding, we forgot that we were hiding and we forgot what we were seeking. We sort of liked the adrenaline rush of being on our own, separate to make our mistakes and reap our successes.

We so liked it that it began to stick. The seeking shifted from looking for love and oneness and remembering the Truth even in the midst of illusion, to seeking something outside of ourselves. This seeking took us to other people, to money, to success and fame, to survival even. Over time, all memory of the Truth, our Oneness with all that is, was buried so deep that we couldn't find it even when we remembered to try.

We instead built up false identities. Ones that would have us know lack, limitation, aloneness, unworthiness. We came to believe that we were not enough, that we were unlovable and different than everyone else. Now, as we let that go and instill a new foundation, we come to know our Selves, we know oneness, abundance, expansion and worthiness. We know we are enough, loved and lovable. We discover that we are unstoppable in our expression of love and light. We learn to live not from the past or in the future, but fully present, right here and right now, to whatever is happening.

Present Moment

The present moment is called that because it is a gift. The past is over and the future has not come yet. Most of us live in either the past or the future. Very few people are totally present in the present. When you find someone who is, you feel Presence.

Presence is an energy vibration of being present, not only to the moment, but to the deeper parts of ourselves. Presence comes when body, mind and spirit are in alignment. It comes when the emotional and mental body are in alignment with the spiritual body. Presence comes with integrity, authenticity, compassion and love.

Presence is a gift and it can be cultivated. Presence brings peace, no matter what is happening in the outer world. Presence is power. Presence is beauty and radiance. Presence is like a rare stone and when you encounter it, it calls you to be a better version of yourself.

Presence is cultivated and developed as a byproduct of spiritual practice and alignment. Presence happens when the consciousness is cleared out enough that one can be totally present to what is happening by allowing, accepting and appreciating each moment.

Until then, the emotions, the limits, the outer conditions dictate the moment. Would you rather be run by outer circumstances or be in total awareness of your Self? Seems like the answer is simple, yet it comes down to a choice that most of us are unwilling to take. Why is that? It's habit, it's cultural conditioning, it's easier to be a victim to life than 100% responsible for it.

How do you make another choice? Find ease in every moment. Find the way to breathe enough to create space enough to allow enough to Be. Simply Be. Simply be, without reaction or resistance, without limitations or preconceived notions about what that might mean.

23

Self-Esteem - Coming To Love Yourself

Do you like yourself? No, really, take a moment and listen to the question deeply. Do you like yourself? All of you? Your personality? Your weight? The way you show up in the world in the many roles that you have? But even more importantly, do you like yourself when you wake up in the middle of the night? Do you like yourself in the middle of a struggle? When you are alone? When you are in a group?

Here's a little secret. Most of us do, but many of us do not. We don't like ourselves. It's epidemic. I had lunch the other day with a long time, dear friend. I've known her for over 22 years, closely, deeply, personally. She confessed in our time together that she really did not like herself, in fact she wondered even why she was on the planet. Instead of liking herself, she said she despised herself. Wow, I thought, that's so curious. I wonder what caused that. Then I wondered what the impact of having those feelings had on her life. So we explored it, I dove deep and she was willing to go with me.

Why? What does that mean? Where did you realize this about yourself? We will call her Lily for privacy's sake.

Lily told me about how over the past year, she had become less and less content with her life. She recalls being very content, sitting on her porch, enjoying life to the fullest. Then one day, she woke up filled with discontent.

I asked her what had happened during that year. She had become a full time care giver for a member of her family who was quite possibly terminally ill. That family member is now returning to health and vitality and just in the few days prior to our conversation had moved out of Lily's home to return to her own, after nearly 10 months of intense medical intervention.

Basically Lily had lost herself to the point that in her words, she had discovered that she was a fake. That virus went so deep that it was threatening her well-being and her very. She found herself to be fake in her relationships, in her life, in every way and it was killing her with shame and embarrassment. In fact, in our time together, it was the first time she had ever said that out loud.

Instead of going into the gory details of Lily's experience, take a look at your own life. Are there ways that you feel fake? Are there places that you know you withhold from the world, to keep the peace, to not rock the boat, to maintain status quo? I'm sure there are and in fact, I see a place I can look at within myself.

When we walk through life and especially when we walk tough situations we take on patterns and habits and ways of being that are designed to protect us, that are designed to get us through the rough times. They are barriers. They are cloaks. They are buffers to the deepest, darkest fears and emotions that we are not able to process through in the midst.

This is designed on purpose, and it is a good design. The problem, however, is that when the immediate stress or danger is past, we don't go back and remove the protection. We keep layering on top of it. Eventually, we have so many layers on top of our essence we can't remember who we are.

How do you begin to remove these layers? First of all, if you are in, or have been in, a particularly traumatic situation, get the professional help you might need. We are not meant to walk through trauma alone. See a therapist, a minister, a counselor, or other trained professional to help guide you through.

Who are you? Where are you? I coached Lily to begin exploring the dark and shame-filled places, the very ones that threatened to drown her. I offered to be her lifeline as she took these first steps to discovering who she really is.

We have to unpack what is packed down into the subconscious. We have to pull the weeds out of the garden plot before we can plant the plants we want there. I remember living in Arizona many years ago. I had bought a cute little house with a beautiful, but small yard. I kept it nice and neat and groomed. However, I had one side of the house that was narrow. Between the house and the cinderblock wall there was perhaps 8 feet. I didn't use it, didn't pay any attention to it at all. It was dirt and not of much use.

One day, I went over to it and noticed that the small weeds that had covered the ground had grown--to the tune of 4 feet tall. My side dirt patch had become a jungle of weeds. It was crazy and I didn't really see it coming.

Can you imagine that I wanted to now plant roses in that area? Could I simply dig a hole in the weeds and plant a bush? Of course, it was possible, but would it grow and thrive? Most likely not. First I would need to clear out the jungle. Not only by cutting down the 4 feet tall growth, but also by removing the roots and caring for the soil.

The soil in this example is the soul and the subconscious. It is extremely difficult to plant a rose garden on top of a jungle. It is extremely difficult to plant new beliefs of self-love and appreciation over shame, guilt and deep dark fear.

It is quite possible, however, to remove the weeds of shame, guilt and fear, freeing the area and clearing the field, tilling the soil for the highest likelihood of harvest.

How do you clear it? First, know that it is there. "Oh my, look at my weed jungle." Release judgment of it. You can beat yourself up, feel embarrassed about it, guilty for not handling it earlier or shame even. Or you can simply accept that it is there and now you see it. Once you see it, you can now begin to clear it.

One simple method of clearing is likened to clearing out a garden. Please, remember if you are stuck here, it may be very important to have some professional assistance. *(This is my specialty; you can find my contact information at the end of the book. My signature system quickly, easily and gently removes life-long limiting patterns and beliefs and dissolves invisible glass ceilings so you can have the clarity, confidence and clear direction to live the life of your dreams.)*

Back to Lily. As she is willing to tell the truth that she despises herself and she is a fake, she is empowered to begin the clearing process. "Oh look, here is a waist high field of weeds, let's clear it out!" Yes, I'm making light of this scenario. In part, because this is such a serious challenge for many of us, but bringing a lightness of spirit and heart can make the path easier.

Become curious. Ok, so you don't like yourself. Really? Why? When did that begin? Who are you beneath this belief? Can you accept that you don't like yourself? Can you go to, "I totally love the part of me that doesn't like me?" Or can you become willing to love the part of you that doesn't like you? Can you even begin to imagine either in the future or the past, a time when you did like yourself? What was that like? How was it different?

Very often, there will be a conversation like: "but you don't know how bad I am," or "you don't know what I've done..." Cool, want to tell me? Ok. "I love you. You are lovable. You are loved." Tell me more. Who are you deep inside there? What is your secret hope or dream? Let's activate that and clear what comes up around it.

When we take on responsibility that may or may not be ours to do, but we forget ourselves in the process of that, we do get lost. Our hearts get buried, our needs get put aside, and our ability to put ourselves first gets forgotten. If you don't take care of yourself first, you won't have anything left to give to others.

The first rule in care-taking is to take care of yourself first. It's so important to get caretaker support. Take time to nurture yourself. Take time to rest, nourish your body, mind and spirit. Take time to remember who you are, outside of the role you find yourself in.

For Lily, she gets to remember what makes her heart sing. She gets to choose again and again to like and love herself, even in the midst of the experience of despising herself. It feels like an oxymoron, but it works. Remember to ask yourself why you believe what you believe and that feelings are only energy in motion – let them flow. Even when they feel ugly. Tell the truth about what you are experiencing. Do it in a safe place and then choose again.

By the way, Lily has come to not only like herself again, but to truly love herself. She still has moments when she wants to forget, but she has enough tools and experience now to catch herself and come back to love. She is loving her life and doing what brings her joy. When she has to go back into care-taking mode, which does happen, she does not lose herself in it. She is totally present and then takes care of herself first, so she can be present to her charge!

Choose love. Choose peace. Choose gratitude. Find it, memorize it and it will change your life. I promise!

24

Finding Ease in the Better

When things are tough and get a little better, there comes a sense of relief. Better is better than what was currently happening. Better lifts us up along the emotional scale. The work, if there is any, is to move on up the scale and feel better and better! Movin' on up, reminds me of the *Jefferson*'s Theme Song, "*Moving On Up to the East Side*". Moving on up to the High Side!

"Better" gives us an opening, an expansion, if only a tiny little bit. It provides the rip in the veil, the crack in the closed door, the glimmer of light shining through. Just a little bit better, gives us relief and a sense of greater ease. Perhaps it's not easy yet, but finding ease is the beginning.

And when we move into better, we have begun. If we find ourselves in a deep dark closet of our life, in pain or fear or anger, we are prisoners to the dark. But and when we crack open the door, even just a tiny, little crack, the light can begin to shine.

Darkness cannot take away darkness,
only light can do that. - Martin Luther King

Light doesn't judge the darkness, it doesn't argue with it, it doesn't make deals with it. The light does nothing to the darkness other than replace it. When we move into or towards the light, all things are possible.

It is said we are either growing or dying. We are either moving into more life or less life. We, as energy beings, are never stagnant. Another way to put it is that we are always either contracting or expanding.

An easy test is to ask yourself, when making a decision is this: Is it expansive or contracting? You can feel it in your body. You know it. Even a good idea can be contractive, if it is not believable or too far from reach.

Look for anything that causes relaxation in your body and expansion in your heart and energy fields.

Try it. Stand up, if you can. Stand in the middle of your room and turn around. Look at what you see and notice what you notice. Feel a sense of contraction, feel the weight of the world on your shoulders, let your body collapse a bit and shrug down. Notice how that is for you. What do you think and feel in this place? When you are ready, stand up tall, throw your shoulders back, lengthen your spine and take a step across an invisible line into an expanded place. Notice how you feel now? Taller? Stronger? Freer? What else?

Look at the beautiful sky. Look at the big, expansive, almost infinite, but certainly finite sky. What can you see? Do you see blue? Grey? Clouds? Airstreams? Do you see tree tops? As I sit here on my porch having my writing time, I see the bright blue of an Arizona sky. I see the tops of rows upon rows of palm trees, hanging out up there in the deep blue. It makes me happy. It makes me expansive. How about you?

For contrast look down at your lap if you are sitting, at your feet if you are standing. Narrow your view to see only the ground beneath your feet. Let your energy contract into only seeing what is there. Today, I see a big, uncomfortable, bulky boot that is supporting a healing ankle. I see toenails on the other foot that are getting very close to needing a new pedicure and coat of polish. I see no possibilities here today, only frustration, disappointment and a sense of being immobile. Immobile is both logistical and figurative as I look down.

If we take this idea bit further, the other thing you can see is your challenge, your current life situation. It is a very narrow view point and limiting. What is that thing that catches your attention? The thing that you want, but when you think about it, all you can think about is what you don't want. For example, I want healing in this ankle that I sprained 10 weeks ago. Yet when I look down, all I can see and focus on is why hasn't it healed, now I have to spend three more weeks in this dang boot, and I miss my flip flops. I'm stuck, I'm limited.

Do you see what happened? I begin thinking about what I wanted: Healing. Then immediately I got sucked into that which I don't want, the opposite of what I think I want.

Think about what you want, what you would love. Look down and see that it feels hard or impossible, even. See how the opposite of what you want seems to appear when we look down. See the ground beneath your feet. Now look up. Look up to eye level. See the room you sit in, or see what is out the window in front of you. Notice that you can see more. Then look up to the sky. Notice what happens in your body when you lift your eyes and your head. Notice what happens to your thinking when you look up.

The simple act of lifting our eyes and head activates hormones and chemicals in our physical bodies and opens us to something new.

Take it another step deeper. Activate your challenge. Maybe you want to travel and when you think about traveling, all you see is how you can't do it. You don't have the time, the money, the freedom and it is out of your reach. Perhaps, you even talk yourself out of it with reasons and excuses. Let it be there, whatever it is. Allow it, acknowledge it and accept what you see. This is not a time of judgment, only of observation.

Fully activated in your experience, look down once more. Notice that you can only see a certain distance when you look down. It's pretty small. Now, raise your eyes and look up. Eye level first and notice what you notice. Then look up to the sky. Lift your eyes and lift your head. Lifting your head actually activates the neck muscles and triggers new neuropathways of possibilities! As you look up, see or imagine yourself in the countries you want to visit, see the travel schedule, the hotels, feel the change in culture. Imagine it, feel it.

Look up to the sky, whether it is a pretty sky or not, it does not matter. Look up to the Sun and feel your expansion. Looking up activates the front of your throat, physiologically and neurologically. There is a science in eye position and relaxation or activation. I'm not going to go into it here, but know that it exists and has been proven effective.

Notice that your vision has already expanded. That the pure area of your sight is exponential from where you were looking down. You can see miles, perhaps. Now spend a moment aware of all that you can see, and all that you cannot see. The biosphere, the atmosphere, the light miles of space between you and the sun. Imagine seeing the sun and the other planets in our galaxy. Imagine seeing the Milky Way. Then go further, out beyond our galaxy, beyond our universe to infinity.

Imagine now, that you are out there looking back upon our galaxy, upon our earth and solar system. Imagine being able to see the planet as a little blue marble spinning through eternity. Then focus in onto your continent, your country, your city and see it from afar. Allow your life to come into your vision. See it as an observer. See the many paths of possible solutions. See yourself making a choice to move forward, to no longer stay stuck in your problem or your life.

The simple physical and figurative act of looking up frees us from bondage. It opens us, expands us to a new possibility. We will only get what we can believe or see. When we lift our heads, we can open to another possibility, we expand so we can see something new. As you look up, allow your mind to wander, allow your physical body to relax, allow your spirit to soar. Bask here with no agenda for as long as you can then notice what you notice. Perhaps you land on a new idea, a possibility, a twist in your road. Either way, you have expanded your consciousness from a limited perspective to an expanded one by looking up.

25

Its Your Life - When are You Going to Live it???

It's time to come alive. We've been living these lives like zombies, going through the motions like a black and white TV show. My husband and I watched the movie *Pleasantville* the other night. It's a beautiful story of moving from "everything is pleasant" to "full and living color". It's time to WAKE UP to the glory that you are! It's time to infuse your life with joy, sizzle, glitter and the nectar of life.

Do something every single day that you love. It could be as simple as drinking a cup of coffee outside on your deck or patio, taking the time to really relish the taste and the moment. It could be having a conversation with a loved one or a stranger. Maybe it is putting color on paper, dancing or other creative expression. What is it for you? What little, small action can you take today to begin to tap into the essence and qualities of a life more fulfilled?

What actions can you plan to take in the next month or year? Begin them now. If you want to take a course, get the course description. If you want to travel, begin to research the travel guides or pick up a brochure of a place you want to visit.

Begin to live with the question, "What would I love?" Ask yourself all day, every day. Notice the themes that are arising and the voices right behind them. Activate the themes, and clear the resistance, reasons, excuses and very soon you will be living the life you love!

Powerful Beyond Measure

You are here to make manifest the glory of yourself. It is not the darkness that frightens you, it is our power. We looked at an excerpt of Marianne Williamson's poem earlier. Here it is in its complete form:

> **"Our deepest fear is not that we are inadequate. Our deepest fear is that we are powerful beyond measure. It is our light, not our darkness that most frightens us. We ask ourselves, Who am I to be brilliant, gorgeous, talented, fabulous? Actually, who are you not to be? You are a child of God. Your playing small does not serve the world. There is nothing enlightened about shrinking so that other people won't feel insecure around you. We are all meant to shine, as children do. We were born to make manifest the glory of God that is within us. It's not just in some of us; it's in everyone. And as we let our own light shine, we unconsciously give other people permission to do the same. As we are liberated from our own fear, our presence automatically liberates others."**
>
> **- Marianne Williamson**

What keeps you from expressing your greatness? What is your greatest fear? Why do you fear it? Does it cause you to suffer? If so, would you be willing to pull it out and look at it? Would you be willing to drop it? If you are unable to by yourself, would you be willing to get support?

What is that one thing that keeps you stuck where you are? Ask yourself the question and allow an answer to arise from the depths of your being. It will be simple and it might surprise you. What is it? Would you be willing to let it go? To do whatever it takes to shift it, so you can have the life you'd love to live?

What if you were powerful beyond measure? What happens with that thought? Who are you to be brilliant, gorgeous, talented, fabulous? Actually, who are you not to be? What if you stepped in to the Truth of who you are here to be? What if you recognized that most of your suffering comes from NOT being that, and being distracted by life instead? Who might you be? Could you come out in a new way and live a life of ease?

Feel into your Yes! And notice the places that are screaming, "No!" Just notice and become curious once again. Can you claim a new life? Can you begin to imagine what life would be like if you claimed your brilliance? It's a game changer for sure! As you lean into the deeper impulse within you, ideas will come, pathways will open and opportunities will arise that support the You that you are becoming and the life you'd love living.

When Life Sucks...

Let's be clear. Sometimes life simply sucks. Even when you know better and you understand that all things work together for a greater good, even then, most of us have times when Life Sucks. My friend, Cathy who has had no children, but has always had pets that were like her children, lost her beloved best friend dog of 16+ years who died. Cathy is heartbroken and devastated. For her, today, life sucks.

A colleague of mine just heard that her daughter was murdered this morning while she was dropping off her kids at school, by her ex-boyfriend, who then killed himself. The kids who are 3 and 5, were injured, and will be ok physically. But they watched their mom be killed and will be emotionally impacted by this for the rest of their lives. The mom is dead, the ex is dead and the grandmother, my colleague is devastated. Not to mention all of the other young children, teachers and parents who witnessed this violent crime, who will all have to live through this moment. Sometimes there is very real suffering and life totally sucks.

A young woman I know gave birth to her first child - a beautiful baby girl, born with genetic defects to her heart and lungs. They did not know it until her birth. She died only a few weeks later. The mom and dad were outside on their patio, rocking the baby, with mom singing "Over the Rainbow" when she died. That is heart wrenching pain, mixed with exquisite beauty in sacred moments.

When life totally sucks - get help. Take care of yourself! Remember to eat and sleep. Reach out to your friends and family. Take the next breath and then the next. Feel the feelings, talk about your experience as you can. Get help again. We are not meant to go through life alone and in the midst of extreme suffering, it is easy to isolate. Throughout this book we have been talking about eliminating suffering and struggle. In times like these, do not rush through it. Feel it, struggle with it, experience it and keep breathing. Put one foot in front of the other. You will get through it. I know you will. I know my friends will, but that does not discount the suffering of today.

If someone you know is in deep suffering, sit with them, hold their hand. Tell them you are here with them. Do not read them this book – it's not for them right now. It's for you. Tell them you love them. Ask them what they need. Take them food and a nice soft comfort blanket.

If your life doesn't totally suck today, that's wonderful! My friend who had the knee surgery is doing fantastic and she definitely has moments when life sucks! For her, she is well on a healing journey and sees progress every day, and it still sucks. The physical pain sucks. The immobility sucks. The reliance on other people sucks. And yet it doesn't. For her, she is learning a deeper compassion and appreciation. For her, she is learning to receive and to rest. There are beautiful gifts in her process.

What doesn't kill you makes you stronger. This too shall pass. Everything works together for a greater good. Are these platitudes or truth statements? Yes, would be the answer. What sucks is when someone outside of you is telling you to be different than you are. What sucks is to have your feelings and experiences discounted. "Oh you shouldn't feel that way. That's wrong." That sucks.

Bring your energy back to yourself and tell the truth. What are you feeling? What are you experiencing? What is going on in your head and body? Face it and name it, even if it is resentment towards the person telling you to be different.

You have my permission and encouragement to feel everything, to pull it out, isolate it and name it. This is not blatant permission to act badly or inappropriately.

Sometimes life sucks. There you have it. Now you can move on. What would you love instead? What can you do in the midst of it sucking? Identify one simple action you can take. That's it. Then choose. Do you want to stay here or do you want to experience something other than sucking? Either way, it's ok. It's just a choice.

Given that life sucks. Now what? Given that it is raining on my hike day, now what? Given that my pet died, now what? Given that life sucks, now what?

You have total and complete choice in how to respond to life, when you remember that you do. When you stop and take a look at what's really happening inside of you, then you can choose. You can also choose to not accept it - but that causes immediate suffering and resistance to what is.

Life sucks, I'm going for a walk to find something I like. I hear a bird, I let that distract me from my suckiness. I look up. I look around. Yes, this sucks. Or does it?

26

Closing Thoughts

I am committed to the end of struggle and suffering. I know that life can get easier. I know there is a deep meaning to life and that you are meant to be fulfilled, to be joy-filled and alive with the possibilities of life. I know that you are meant for great things and that as you free your soul, you will discover a depth to your own Being-ness that right now, might not seem like a possibility at all.

My friend tells a story of being very close to a huge life-changing goal when he got stuck. He was selling his heart out, moving close to breaking through a bar that few people in his company were reaching. Then everything stopped. He quit selling. He couldn't sell anything. For a week, then another and another. The time was running short and he was blanking. He began to wonder what was really going on. In a "no-kidding" kind of way. What was happening?

Ultimately, he asked for help. His colleague suggested that he invest in a session with a coach who, happened to be coming to town in the next few days. He said: "Yes, I'll do whatever it takes!" Then he was told the price and his first reaction was, "I can't do that! I don't have that kind of money, I just tanked for the past three weeks."

The question his colleague asked him in that moment was "What would it be worth to you, to reach this goal? What would it be worth to you to master this life principle? To know once and for all how to keep going and not get stuck." Oh, that is priceless.

So he invested in himself and discovered a hidden barrier to his success. He was able to break though that barrier and not only achieve his sales goal, but crush it! He sold twice what he needed to, far surpassing his goal in the remaining three weeks he had.

He says now, that the intellectual knowledge was good, but the experience and integrated knowing in his body has changed his life. It was a game changer and everything improved. Everything has changed by blasting through his hidden barriers of belief and opening the pathway to greater success.

I'm here to tell you, there is one simple thing that can change your entire world. Find it, shift it, eliminate it and replace it with a greater truth and you are on your way. You might be asking, "is there only one thing?" No, probably not. But once you shift the one, the others become more apparent and easier.

The simple thing to do and remember every time is to move from an energetic sense of contracting to expansion. Do whatever you can to shift from tight to open, from tense to relaxed. In this book, you have been given many techniques and tools to use to make those shifts.

And these are the tip of the iceberg. There is so much more. More expansion, more light, more love, more joy, more purpose, more passion, more connection available. It is here for you and I'd love to assist you in receiving it!

If you have enjoyed this book, please share it, pass it along. Tell your friends. You may join my online community by signing up for my emails, by joining my fb group and liking my page. Links are found in the following section. To learn even more, go to:

www.AlizaBloom.com

And in case you didn't know, I've created a companion book, *Falling Into Ease Guidebook – Simple Everyday Practices to Release Suffering and Create Ease In Your Life*. You can find it on the Amazon store.

I also invite you to join me in our Facebook Group,
Falling Into Ease HERE:
https://www.facebook.com/groups/248840942168324/

I have so enjoyed writing this for you! I hope you have enjoyed reading and applying the principles as much as I have. I'd love to hear from you! Email me here: aliza@alizabloom.com

About the Author

Aliza's first book, *Be a BOA, Not a Constrictor*, available as an eBook on Kindle, is an inspired fable for authentic transformation, becoming BOA; Bold, Outrageous, Authentic. She also is a contributing author in the Best Selling 365 Series, *365 Ways to Connect with Your Soul,* and *365 Moments of Grace.*

Aliza has a presence of deep peace, quiet joy, unbridled listening and quickness of mind. She brings a light touch to life even as she is fierce in her stand for you. As a speaker and facilitator she commands the room with presence, humor and passion.

Thanks for reading my book!

I created a meditation to accompany the deep heart exploration you will experience as you fall into ease. You may download that as my gift to you HERE:

http://alizabloom.com/ease-meditation-freebie/

Resources

Page 67: To listen to the conversation we had with Bob and Noel here: www.cocreatorsconvergence.com/#!2016-archives/c1smj

How to Work with Me

If you have been inspired by the tips, tools, techniques and stories of this book and want personalized help to end your own suffering, here are some ways to connect with me:

Learn more about me here:
www.AlizaBloom.com

Join My Virtual Community
Facebook: https://facebook.com/revaliza/

Falling Into Ease Facebook group: https://www.facebook.com/groups/248840942168324/

Twitter: https://twitter.com/AlizaBloom

LinkedIn: https://www.linkedin.com/in/aliza-bloom-robinson-58970b24